All Together You

by Bette DeHaven
in collaboration with Ruth Milliron

INTERNET SERVICES CORPORATION, CHARLOTTE, NC

Acknowledgements

This book is definitely a combined effort. So many wonderful people have helped make it possible. Ruth Milliron, my sister, collaborated and critiqued the entire effort. She deserves the entire credit for Chapter 9 on "Let's Go Shopping". Her God-given talent in the area of fashion co-ordination has been a great inspiration to me. My husband's patience and help were so necessary. My associate, Sue Cappelen, was and is such an encouragement to me.

The creativity and ideas of Penny Onley, Sherry Collins and the whole designLINE team were invaluable in presenting this book. The illustrations, done by Betty Ruhl, made it all come alive. I appreciate the faith the Yagers have in me; it made this book possible.

Last, but certainly not least, I thank my heavenly Father for giving me the desire, the persistence and the people mentioned above to bring this book to completion.

Thank you each and every one!

Bette DeHaven

Contents

Forward

   This book provides women with some excellent guidelines and principles in the area of their image development. It includes everything from the foundation of color to ways to compliment their total look and uniqueness of style.

   Personal style rarely comes effortlessly or even naturally. Many women, from a very young age, know what type of clothing they like, whether it is sporty or romantic, etc. The development of these preferences into good personal style takes a knowledge of what looks good and how to put it together successfully. Personal style is an invention or a creation born to each individual woman. Therefore, good taste and judgement must be learned and developed, and then exercised in choosing fashions that best express who you are.

   There are some dangers we encounter when we shop for ourselves. One is the attempt to imitate someone else's look or style. Because no two people are exactly alike, unless you are an identical twin, you can never look the way that person does in her clothes and accessories. Role models are important but not for carbon copying because you will usually look like a counterfeit!

   Have you ever tried on an outfit exactly the way it was displayed? Were you disappointed with the way it looked on you? That is because the outfit was not chosen for you. In fact, some things only look good on display!

Another pitfall to good style is in trying to overcome negative feedback received in past years, particularly the teenage years. In many instances, you forsake who you really are to become something or someone you are not.

In this book, we will consider the following components of good personal style:

1. Your physical characteristics (coloring, hair type, body frame and proportions)

2. Your clothing personality (your inner attitudes and preferences)

3. Your wardrobe planning skills and shopping habits

I have worked in the image field for 16 years. What I share in the following pages is a result of what I have observed and learned about women's needs and how to best meet those needs while building a positive and successful image, both inside and out. Just remember, successful people are not intimidated by what they don't know. They act on what knowledge they already have and are always looking for growth opportunities. A successful image develops with a woman's growth and continues to develop throughout her life.

About The Authors...

Bette DeHaven

Bette DeHaven, owner of the California-based company **Designer's Touch**, has over 17 years of experience in all areas of the color and image industry.

Bette obtained her formal education in clothing and textiles from Ohio Wesleyan University and East Texas State University. She also minored in art and design.

Through the years Bette has given thousands of private consultations and presented programs to various professional groups and institutions such as banks, colleges, law firms, churches and plastic surgeons. In addition to her continuous performance in these areas, she has developed and presently directs seminars for **The Crowning Touch**® and **Expressions In Color**, national image organizations.

Ruth Milliron

Ruth Milliron is the owner of **Embellir Custom Cosmetics and Salons**. She is also author of **Spring and Fall Fashion Perspectives**, seasonal style catalogs. For the past 15 years, Ruth, a Certified Color and Image Consultant, has instructed numerous clients in all areas of Image Development. Ruth also consults on an individual basis, creates seasonal style shows and lectures nationally.

She received her bachelor of science degree in clothing textiles and design from Bowling Green State University, where she has served as an administrator for the past 20 years.

1
Where Do You Begin?

The foundation for good image is color. As a result, much has been written, publicized and said about the benefits of color analysis. Today, many women have even had their "colors done" several times because they were dissatisfied with the original results. Sometimes it is at the urging of a friend, or perhaps just because it's fun – especially if it doesn't cost anything and a "make-up party" is involved.

Does any of this sound familiar? The sad thing is that the end result, because of differing opinions each time, is frustration and/or a discrediting to the whole field of color analysis in the mind of the "victim".

So, how do you decide who is right or where to go for an accurate color analysis? The following are some criteria you should consider when determining the credibility of an analyst.

1. A good color analyst recognizes that the **skin response to color is the key** to determining seasonal colors. The response of the natural hair color and eyes to having particular colors draped under an individual's face and across the shoulders must also be considered.

2. A good analyst seeks to choose colors that lift up and promote her client's face and, at the same time, create harmony with all her natural attributes. For example, the client may have a soft ash hair color and a pinky-transparent quality to her skin; bold colors will only overpower this person, whereas soft, dusty, cool-based colors will enhance her completely. Warm colors tend to give her an unhealthy, aged appearance.

3. A good analyst is careful to use natural or simulated "natural" lighting. Care should be taken to make sure the light is evenly diffused on the face, eliminating any unnatural shadows. Auxiliary lighting that has a direct influence should be turned off.

4. A good analyst uses color drapes that have proven to be good test colors. These drapes should represent each of those hues which consistently show well on everyone. For example, the best pink or peach tone, the best blue tone, the best green, brown or black tone, the best red or white tone, and so on. An excellent test between a winter person and a summer person is charcoal gray versus charcoal blue gray or true red versus summer red.

5. The best testing process is to first determine whether your client has a cool blue-based undertone or a warm yellow-based undertone. Rose-pink versus orange is the best test. Once this is done, it can be determined which seasonal pal-ette of color is best in her undertone. I find this procedure to be more accurate and it results in fewer mistakes. The consultant should also help her client see her skin's responses to the test colors as draping occurs.

6. A good analyst recommends the colors that give the most healthy, flawless, appearance to the skin, makes the eyes sparkle and adds richness to the natural hair color.

7. If the hair color has been changed or oxidized by perm or sun, then it must be covered to prevent a false indication with the drape colors. All too often redness or golden qualities in the hair are the results of external influences, rather than inborn traits. Too many clients and consultants make incorrect observations by choosing warm colors that enhance this "unnatural" feature.

I was incorrectly analyzed the first time because, when I was 24 years old, I made myself a golden blonde. When I was draped, I told the consultant my natural brown hair had reddish highlights. As a result, I was draped as a Spring. However, I am a Winter.

8. A good analyst teaches her client proper skin care and make-up techniques and recommends the best color choices for her cosmetics.

9. A good analyst re-drapes her client after cosmetics are applied, verifying the rightness of the colors chosen and allowing her client to see how wonderful this complete harmony with color, cosmetics and her natural attributes can be. At this point in the consultation, the analyst should give personal recommendations as to the best colors and the least flattering colors in her seasonal palette. Not everyone in the same seasonal palette is able to wear all colors equally well, therefore everyone's palette is personal.

The preceding information should be supplied to you if you are paying for a complete color/make-up consultation.

Remember, you will receive the best results from someone who is a trained color consultant, not a "make-up" consultant. If you find the "consultant's" major emphasis is to sell you a product, beware.

10. A good color analyst should have received a minimum of 16 hours of in-depth seasonal color training where she had the opportunity to do hands-on draping and also observed a large number of people draped. Instructional information is not nearly enough by itself. Also, videos are not a substitute for live models! Too many TV's do not have good color balance.

11. A good color analyst should have gone through a color certification test. Obviously, this criteria is also important when choosing someone to train you in color analysis. Don't pay for a color consultation without finding out what and how the service will be rendered, along with the consultant's background and training. Even the best are in danger of becoming lax at times. This is a field where consultants must keep their techniques fine-tuned. I believe "if you don't use it, you can loose it." Realizing this fact, a good training firm will offer refresher courses to their consultants. Experience is a great teacher, but newer consultants can easily get onto a "wrong track" in their draping.

People are not necessarily drawn to colors that compliment them. Because we are emotional beings, we respond to color both physiologically and psy-chologically. So our experiences greatly influence our choices. I do find that more women prefer cooler colors than warm, and that more men prefer warm colors than cool – until such time as their education and experience is broadened. Individuals who do not have good self-esteem will shy away from bold blue-based colors unless they have been conditioned as a child to be positive toward these colors. Obviously then, we can not depend upon our emotions in this realm but we must be open to good, objective advice.

My approach to color analysis is based on the four season theory because it provides an easy-to-understand, effective way to develop a disciplined ward-robe. When the characteristics of each of the four seasonal palettes are explained to have a direct relationship to the four seasons of the year, people can visualize the qualities of these color palettes more readily. Over the years, this technique has been used by several image companies, and each has adapted it to their particular philosophy. However, I am quite a purist when it comes to separating season color bases, chromas, and values.

Winter hues are pure, clean, bold, and sharply contrasting. They are true primary or blue-based in undertone. Just visualize clean, new-fallen snow resting on wet, dark tree bark and pine needles, then contrast this against the crisp, deep blue sky of a winter day – then you have the essence of the winter color palette.

Summer hues are soft, dusty, grayed and have a blue-based undertone. Now visualize a summer day. The sun shines more directly overhead causing the colors to become softer, especially if the humidity levels are high. A misty quality takes over the color of the sky and landscape. When you think of flowers like sweet peas, snap dragons, stock, etc., you can see the qualities of summer pinks, lavenders, white, etc.

Spring hues are clean, clear and somewhat delicate in quality, but with a yellow-base or undertone. Freshness and clarity are the qualities of color this time of year. As you visualize springtime, all color, whether green, red, yellow or blue, seems to be warmed by the bright sunlight. It's especially easy to visualize the budding of new life in the springtime with its yellow-green quality.

Autumn hues are warm, rich, earthy and mellow with a golden undertone in the yellow-base side of color.

Picture New England trees that are breathtaking in all their golden, orange and red hues. As the sun sets, the landscape glows with a warmth unequaled by anything I have ever seen.

As we consider individuals and their seasonal palettes, we must look for the same undertone in their hair, skin, and eyes as we find in the colors which promote, compliment and harmonize their coloring. In other words, a cool or blue undertoned skin must wear a cool or blue undertone color, and a warm or yellow undertone skin must wear a warm or yellow undertone color. Depending upon the depth of the person's coloring, a clear winter palette or soft summer palette will be most complimentary to the cool undertone, and a clear spring palette or an earthy autumn palette will be most complimentary to the warm undertone.

It should be pointed out that surface skin color often disguises the undertone. This is due to melanin, which enables the skin to tan easily. The less melanin, the quicker the skin burns in the sun and the more transparent the skin is. Therefore, olive and darker skins with high melanin content disguise their undertone almost completely; however these individuals are usually blue-based. Many of these skins become sallow; they have a sickly yellow cast with gray shadows as they respond to yellow or golden-based colors. Thus, blue-based colors will bring a healthier quality to this skin, as well as to their hair and eyes.

Many beige skins sallow as well.

The warm skins will sometimes deceive you because they can have a pinky quality in the face, especially if ruddy (high-color). Generally, warm skins are peachy, ivory or coppery in quality.

When I color drape an individual, it is always without make-up. I'm looking for that person to be totally promoted by the color. This means that not only is the skintone complimented by color, but the natural hair color is richer and the eyes are brighter and more alive.

The winter skin will appear brightened and healthy in winter colors. The summer skin will appear soft and somewhat transparent in summer colors. The spring skin will be and must look radiant in spring colors and the autumn skin will appear warm and coppery in the autumn colors.

The wrong colors will dull the skin, hair and eyes. The person usually becomes one with the color, or pulls down into the color, thus aging the face immediately! We must

never lose the person in the color. If the person appears tired, dull and not well, or the skin texture appears coarse, or if the coloring in the face pales and separates into blotchy patches, then the color around the face is definitely wrong. If the attention is drawn to the nose, mouth, chin or jaw, then the color is also wrong.

Good color always lifts the face, drawing attention toward sparkling eyes. The skin looks as though foundation has been re-applied, thus creating a smooth texture and an evenness of color. Not even a facelift can restore the color of youth, but the use of seasonal palettes can greatly enhance a plastic surgeon's work.

Once your season has been determined and you start wearing your colors, you will begin to receive compliments on your appearance. This new, attractive you will result in a new self-confidence as you begin to develop your own sense of personal style.

Characteristics of the Winter Person:

Hair Color:
- Black (blue or brown)
- Brown - dark to medium (warm high-lights, if any are due to sun expo-sure or perms)
- Salt 'n' Pepper - silver or white
- Rarely blonde, but never are they gray (ash) blondes - tend to be more platinum or white blondes.

Many winter children are towheads or white blondes as small children. Some become more honey-colored in adolescence, ultimately turning brown by their adult years. These are sometimes mistaken for Springs!

Note: Winters should always color gray hair with a solid, natural tone if hair coloring is desired.

Skin Tones: (Blue or cool undertone)
- Pale - often blue eyes - of Welsh or Irish descent
- Beige - some are rather sallow with no cheek color

- Rosy - rich in quality
- Olive - light to dark
- Black - light to blue-black tone

Eye Color:
- Shades of brown - light to dark
- Shades of blue - gray-blue to deep blue-violet
- Hazel - two colors in iris
- Shades of green - gray to yellow-green

Note: Yellow or orange in the eyes around the pupil does not mean they are warm. Many Winters have this characteristic.

Eye Patterns:

The typical Winter eye pattern is one with spikes or spokes, most commonly seen in the brown or hazel eye. The spikes, usually black, come off the pupil and may extend to the outer edge of the iris, usually at the top. Some hazel eyes have a heavy orange or yellow splash of color around the pupil. There are other patterns as well, many of which overlap other seasonal characteristics.

Characteristics of the Summer Person:

Hair Color:
- Ash blonde, with gray cast at the base of the hair - may be light to dark
- "Mousy" brown, has a gray cast - looks dull and lifeless in the wrong colors
- Light to dark brown - may have auburn highlights
- Ash gray - silver gray

Note: The ash-toned hair frosts or highlights beautifully.

Skin Tones: (blue or cool undertone)
- Light to deep rose-beige - deeper tones tan nicely
- Very pink to fair with a delicate pink-tone - burns easily
- Pale beige - may sallow a little

Eye Color:
- Blue - clear to gray-blue - aqua.
- Green - gray to yellow-green
- Hazel - pale gray
- Soft brown only, with a gray, rosy cast - no dark brown

Eye Patterns:

The typical Summer eye has a lacy or cracked glass pattern which is created by a webbing effect or tear-drop shapes. Some blue eyes have a very soft opaque appearance with a white effect radiating from the pupil. There are other patterns in the Summer eye which overlap the characteristics of other seasons.

Characteristics of the Spring Person:

Hair Color:
- Blonde - golden to honey
- Strawberry blonde
- Red, several shades - light to deep red
- Golden brown - rarely dark
- Gray - often yellow or dull until fully grown in

NOTE: Blonde hair may be highlighted and red shades are best colored in red tones.

Skin Tones:
(Warm or yellow undertone)
- Ivory to very milky white
- Peachy
- Golden Beige (tanned appearance)
- Ruddy (high color usually in cheeks, chin and forehead)

Eye Color:
- Blue - clear to deep blue
- Green - golden to gray-green or teal
- Hazel - golden brown with green
- Brown - light golden to topaz (not dark)

Eye Patterns:
The typical Spring eye pattern has a sunlight effect coming from a small space or donut shape around the pupil. Sometimes there are some cracked glass shapes in part of the eye. Some Spring patterns closely resemble other seasonal characteristics.

Characteristics of the Autumn Person:

Hair Color:
- Red - strawberry to auburn
- Blonde - honey or drab blonde with gold highlights
- Brown - coppery red-brown - deep chestnut to golden brown
- Golden gray or dull gray
- Charcoal black - dull - not common

Note: Most Autumn hair shades are best colored in the same solid hair color as the natural color.

Skin Tones:
- Ivory or very fair
- Peachy
- Light to dark golden beige - not olive
- Dark beige
- Golden black with a natural bronze-brown hair color
- Ruddy - peachy pink with high color

Eye Color:
- Brown - reddish - very dark to golden amber
- Hazel - brown and blue or brown and green
- Green - cat eye - avocado or pale - clear green
- Turquoise or teal blue - not gray or true blue

Eye Patterns:
The typical Autumn eye pattern is one with a flower petal or star shape around the pupil. There are similarities to some of the cracked glass appearance of the Summer eye.

Any season, warm or cool, may be freckled. Just remember, the cool skins with freckles will appear more blended than the warm skins with freckles; the warm skins are usually more heavily freckled.

I've seen both Springs and Autumns draped as Summers because the consultant's goal was to blend the freckles away. She accomplished her goal, but it was at the expense of taking away the need for radiance in the warm skin. Good healthy color should never be sacrificed just to gain softness. We all need the best of both worlds.

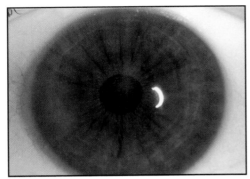

the winter eye

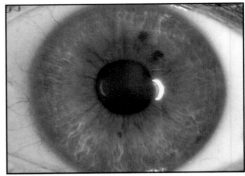

the winter eye

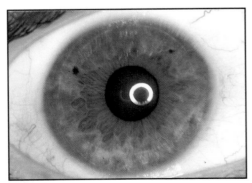

the autumn eye

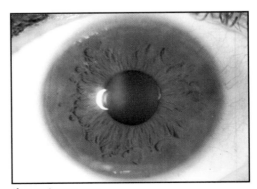

the autumn eye

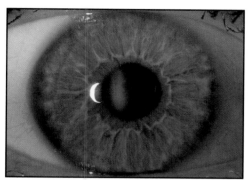

the spring eye

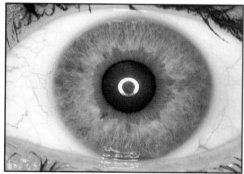

the spring eye

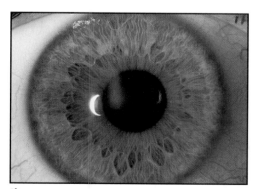

the summer eye

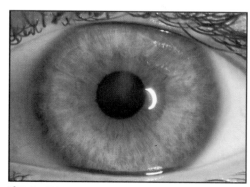

the summer eye

2
What Should You Do With Your Hair?

I can understand how any woman could be frustrated with her hair. When I was younger, mine caused me a great deal of distress at times. I grew up in the '50s, and we didn't have blow dryers, curling irons, mousse, gels, or any of the great styling techniques we have today. My hair is very fine, and as a result, I literally spent hours trying to make it look good. Based on that experience, I am very aware of how important a good hairstyle is to a woman's self-image. Even the Bible states that a woman's hair is her crowning glory.

Women need encouragement and direction with their hairstyles. It's crucial to have a good cut that you can manage by yourself. As a consultant, I have learned everything I can about hair-style and color because I believe it is of utmost impor-tance to my clients and students.

The most com-mon question I get from women is "How do I find a good hairstylist?" It's not easy, but you have to persist.

First, look at the stylist's hairstyle. Is it flattering and current? Do the people who come out of her chair all look the same, or does she take the time to discuss the client's face shape, profile and hair texture? The stylist should handle your hair, play with it, move it to see where your cow-licks and thin spots are located.

Always ask to see photos of styles that are suggested to you. Do you like any of them? Find out how difficult or easy the suggested style is to maintain. If you have no skill or time to duplicate the suggested style, then make sure that you tell your stylist. Many of the techniques used to create style today are really not difficult to learn if you ask for help.

When my stylist changes my style, I use a hand mirror to watch the back as well as the front while she is blow drying and curling my hair. It's important to see how she "picks" or "fingers" your hair into its shape. It is in the stylist's best interest to give you all the help possible because if you look good, your stylist looks good.

Another way to find a good stylist is to look at hair styles when you are in public. It is a compliment to any woman to be stopped and asked where she has her hair done.

A good stylist will update her training at least once a year. She must keep abreast of changing styles and techniques for cutting hair. However, all stylists in a particular salon are not necessarily as good or as updated as the others. Read the magazines and be aware of how styles are changing. Women date themselves very quickly by wearing

an out-of-date hairstyle.

When choosing a hair style among those recommended, your face shape is the first consideration. The perfect face shape is oval; those of us who do not have oval faces strive to achieve the illusion with a flattering hairstyle.

The most important feature of any hair style is that it balances or offsets any imbalance in the face. For example, if you have a long face, then you must add width, not more length, to the face. If you have a triangular or pear-shaped face, then

you must add fullness from the eyes up to balance the lower, wider part of your face.

You should not repeat your face shape with your hair style. No rounded looks on the round face or square looks on the square face, etc. Just apply good principles of balance, based on the shape of your head set and profile. A good stylist will look at these features and discuss them with you.

The right stylist, however, is not necessarily the best colorist. In your very finest salons, whether in Beverly Hills or New York

City, you may visit one person for your hairstyle and another for your color, and still another for a perm. Any beautician who has been licensed by her state has had to pass a test in all three of these areas, but that is still not a guarantee that she is talented in all three. I find that often a gifted stylist, one who is creative and understands proportion and balance, is not able to correctly translate these gifts into the color area; she may tend to be too creative with color.

Creating warm hair color tones is much easier than creating good cool/ash tones — an honest beautician will tell you that. Depending on porosity and texture of the hair, it will lift color at different rates. What works for one situation will not for the next. Whether you like it or not, the first time someone colors your hair, you are often a "guinea pig", depending on the type of hair you have.

If you find a good stylist, it's worth driving 100 miles once a month to receive her services. Don't settle for mediocre, settle only for the best!

Note: There are several things which affect and change your natural hair color. The results may often be warm in appearance.

Hair Color Changes May Result From:

- Permanent hair color treatment
- Semi-permanent hair color application
- Frosting, glazing highlighting
- Sun exposure
- Permanents
- Straightening
- Henna shampoos
- Chlorinated pools
- Well-water (rural areas)
- Medication
- Pregnancy

You need to tell your color consultant if any of these conditions apply to you.

3
Are You Comfortable With Your Body?

Like so many adolescents, I did not like the body God gave me. My waist was too big; my hips were too flat; and my legs were not shapely enough. It seemed as though all my friends had perfect "little" figures. Actually, as I think back, I would have been happier if I had been born in the 1800's when women wore corsets and long, full dresses. That would have disguised all my "flaws"! Well, as I have learned over and over again, God's plan and timing in our lives is always perfect.

Now, I wouldn't change my time and place in the scheme of things for anything.

My flaws have kept me humble and much more able to relate to other women, who are just as critical of themselves as I am of myself. It took many years of my adult life to come to understand that my frame can never be changed, no matter how thin I get or how much exercise I do.

As I worked with color analysis and make up, I realized that was only the beginning of image develop-ment. I would hear retailers complain about "these women with their color charts" coming in to their stores and having no idea about style and line, just wanting anything in the right "color". That prompted me to put together a total image pro-gram. I observed women's shapes and found that there were similari-ties in their overall frame and that there were some basic frames that most bodies re-sembled.

In college, we measured to

determine size and shape, and I came to realize that most women are intimidated by measuring tapes. The thought that other women might know their bust, waist and hip size, especially if their measurements increase as they descend the body, is horrifying! As a Home Economics major, with an emphasis in clothing, textiles and design, I began to see how clothing styles and lines can enhance or destroy any figure. For many years, I sewed and tailored all my clothes, particularly suits and dresses; I learned what lines flattered my figure.

So, my conclusion was that we need to correct what is obviously disproportionate. Most figure problems can be disguised - even excessive weight problems can be minimized visually. Knowing this now makes me want to take each woman I see with a low self-image and say "I can help you!"

Everybody has potential for attractiveness. In fact, there are very few natural beauties, if that is of any comfort. As Jean Lush, author of **Emotional Phases of a Woman's Life,** has said, "Today's woman has no excuse not to be attractive." Never has there been a time in history when women have had so many tools available to create beauty. As recently as 30 years ago, you were either blessed with attractive attributes or you were not. Today's woman, however, can only claim laziness or lack of interest if she has not developed her potential. That's why I'm so glad God placed me in this time frame. I have every possible advantage for hair care, skin care, cosmetics, clothing styles and fabric choices.

Even extra weight is not an excuse for a lack of style and attractiveness. Many women who are overweight feel they do not deserve to spend money on themselves; they punish themselves by looking dumpy. They don't realize they are also punishing those they care about by setting a poor example and lowering their self-image. A vicious cycle develops. Year after year, they talk about losing weight and, because their motivation gradually fails, they never do. Thus the best years of their life pass them by while they wait for the right time and the right diet. Sometimes a cynical attitude is the end result, and this only destroys relationships. I pray this is not your plight. If it is, however, take heart. Begin to develop your look at your current weight. Stop waiting for tomorrow or next year and learn how to dress the body you have and enjoy life today!

Whatever your figure problems, there are good clothing lines for all of them. Don't look to the retail store clerks for good advice. Most sales people will not be honest with you because their first priority is sales for the store. Besides, they do not know you, your personality, lifestyle, etc. In all fairness, there are those exceptional clerks who have a good eye for proportion or who have had some image training. However, these people are definitely in the minority.

Once I learned that I could disguise all the "flaws" that concerned me, I became much less self-conscious and much more people conscious. I forgot about how I look from other angles and directed my thoughts to the task at hand. It is a liberating feeling to learn how to successfully dress your figure.

If you have already found an attractive hairstyle, achieved your best look with cosmetics and learned what colors really compliment you, then the next step in developing your personal style is learning how to balance your figure with good lines and proportion.

4

How Do Clothing Lines and Fabrics Affect Your Figure?

I am amazed at how often women choose clothes that add pounds to their appearance. Principles of good proportion and balance are really very simple; anyone can learn them. So, if you want to look thinner or even heavier, this chapter offers you the answers you are seeking.

There is a tremendous amount of illusion involved in the development of good proportion. The primary goal of any clothing is to create a balanced body. Therefore, the first question you should ask yourself when you try on any garment is "**Does this balance my figure frame or does it call attention to my figure flaws?**"

Line and Proportion

Every garment has three major sets of lines which affect the figure. The first is **body lines** which are created by the seams, darts, tucks, etc. These lines provide the fit and contour of the garment.

The second set of lines are the **silhouette lines;** these are formed by the basic shape of the garment. For example:

- A sheath silhouette creates the illusion of slimness and height unless the garment is closely fitted where there is a figure problem.
- An A-line silhouette will hide a full or wide hip and derriére, slimming the figure. It also balances a full bust or wide shoulders.
- A chemise of unshaped silhouette will cause the figure to look taller, slimmer, and hide a thick waist if need be.

■A blouson or dropped-waist silhouette can balance or conceal problems like a short, thick waist and full bust.

Detail lines are the third set of lines. They are formed by the pattern detail on the garment such as repeated horizontal, vertical or curved lines. As we think of horizontal lines and their effect on the figure, we will see an illusion of width created, and thus a shorter figure. Visualize a shorter figure with lots of horizontal lines. This figure will look shorter and heavier than it actually is, especially if these lines are placed at fuller parts of the body. A singular horizontal line can create the illusion of more height if placed above or below the median line of the body. (See Figure A)

Figure A

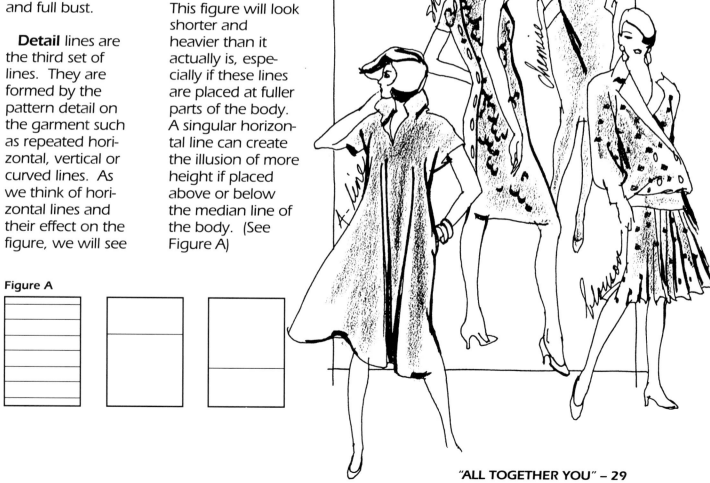

Shoulder yokes will add width across the shoulder or bustline. All hemlines, whether on the skirt, overblouse, jacket or vest, should be at a flattering level — not at a figure problem.

A vertical line usually makes the person look taller and slimmer, particularly if it is a singular line because this leads the eye upward. However, if the vertical line is repeated several times, it can lead the eye horizontally, especially if the lines are not close together. A garment with a singular vertical line down the center front with buttons is very slimming, as well as a solid, unbroken color. (See Figure B)

Other slimming vertical lines include princess seaming, pleats, and gored shapes, depending upon their placement.

Diagonal and curved lines can be very slimming if the angles are deep enough. A shorter angle will give the impression of width. (See Figure C)

Finally, we often forget that a negative line placed at a fuller part of the figure need not be avoided, if we place a positive line at a smaller part of the figure for balance. (See figure on page 29)

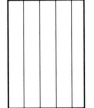 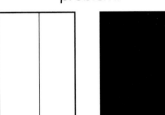

Figure B

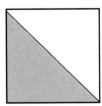

Figure C

The size of the pattern on a garment will affect the appearance of the weight and size of the body. For example, if a figure is surrounded by large items it appears smaller or even dwarfed. But if a figure is surrounded by small items, it appears larger. (See Figure D) So, if a large woman puts on a small print, she will look larger. If a small woman wears a large print, she will look smaller and even overwhelmed. By

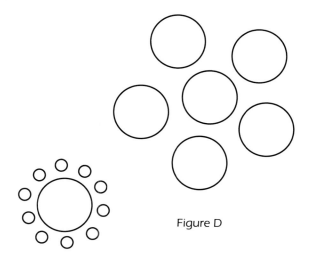

Figure D

Shoulder pads balance peplum ...

the same token, a small face in large earrings will look even smaller and vice-versa. Remember to carry out this principle as you apply jewelry to the body. A large woman needs larger necklaces or pins, nothing small or dainty.

Color and its optical illusions must be considered at the same time. If a large print is placed on a large woman for correct balance, it should not be in bright colors such as red, orange or yellow because these colors increase apparent size and attract the eye first. Contrasting color patterns will do the same thing.

If the colors used are in the blue, green or violet family, they can actually reduce the size of the figure. Muted colors also tend to recede and reduce the apparent figure size.

In our discussion of proportion, we also need to consider fabric. Bulky fabrics such as coarse tweeds, wide wale corduroys, heavy wools and nubby knits will give the impression of added weight. Crisp or stiff fabrics like taffeta, heavy poplin or duck cloth will stand away from the body and hide some imperfections, but again they add the appearance of extra weight if there is much volume to the fabric.

Shiny fabrics like satin or charmeuse reflect light and cause the body to look heavier. On the other hand, matte textures absorb light and are the best choices for the larger figure. Matte fabrics include flat knits, gabardines, crepe, challis, etc. These fabrics are good for every figure, small or large.

Ideally, fabric should hang well on the figure without clinging to any bulges. The more rounded the figure, the drapier the fabric can be; the straighter the figure, the crisper the fabric can be.

Like body weight and shape, hair should also be considered when selecting fabric textures. The wrong fabric weight and/or the wrong shade can destroy a woman's hair texture and color instantly.

As you know by now, proportion is

most pleasing when good overall balance is achieved. It is most pleasing when areas on the figure are unevenly divided to create interest. Examples of this would be found in combinations of jackets or tops with pants or skirts. That is why we see longer jackets with shorter skirts and shorter jackets with fuller pants or long skirts.

As you look at the proportion of any garment, you need to ask if it will flatter your positive features and conceal the negative ones, and you should evaluate the use of color, print, fabric and design.

Major Figure Problems

Now that we have looked at some of the principles of line and proportion, we need to consider the figure and any possible problems. Major figure problems are obvious to others, but, with the right techniques, they can be minimized or

disguised. Here are a few:

1. Long neck

2. Short neck and double chin

3. Round or sloping shoulder (emphasizes extra weight)

4. Broad shoulders

5. Thin arms (bony)

6. Heavy arms or flabby arms

7. Small bust/ flat chest

8. Full/low bust

9. Thick waist

10. Short waist

11. Long waist

12. Protruding tummy (more prominent than bustline)

13. Wide hips (just below the waist)

14. Large upper thighs or saddle-bags

15. Protruding derriére

16. Flat derriére

17. Short legs

18. Thin legs

19. Large calves/ thick ankles

Minor figure problems are noticed only by you and are often imagined to be major problems. The only time someone else notices them is when you tell, and even then that person will probably say she'd never noticed it before! If you learn to do a good job of disguising a major problem, no one else will ever see it unless you verbally call attention to it.

Having identified the major figure problems, let's relate them to one of the four body frames.

A-FRAME

1. Appearance of body is narrower at top half and wider at the lower hip and upper thigh area.

2. May have rounded derriére and be sway-backed.

3. Legs may be shorter and some-times heavier.

4. Upper torso may be average to long; firm and slender.

5. Bust is usually average to small; rarely large.

6. Figure can remain very youthful if there is no tendency to gain weight.

7. Gains first few pounds in the saddlebag area.

Your goal with this frame is to balance it by widening the shoulders. This can be achieved by choosing garments that have shoulder pads or sleeve detailing.

4. Thighs and derriére are usually flat.

5. Legs are normally thin.

6. May have a tummy problem; in fact, may be barrel-shaped around the upper torso.

7. Gains weight in the upper torso area first.

Your goal with this frame is to balance it by widening the hip and upper leg area. This would entail choosing garments that have width and fullness in the skirt or pants.

V-FRAME

1. Shoulders appear to be obviously wider than hips.

2. Is usually large-busted with shorter waist and high hips.

3. Appearance is top heavy.

H-FRAME

1. Body appears to be fairly straight up and down.

2. Thighs and derriére are usually flat.

3. Waist is usually thicker, giving a straighter appearance to figure.

4. Legs may be longer.

5. Bust may be average to large.

6. Weight gain is usually through the middle; waist and tummy before thighs and lower hips.

Your goal with this frame is to balance it by creating the illusion of a smaller waist or disguising it altogether. This can be accomplished by choosing either a bloused garment with a flared skirt and belted waist or a straight garment like a chemise dress.

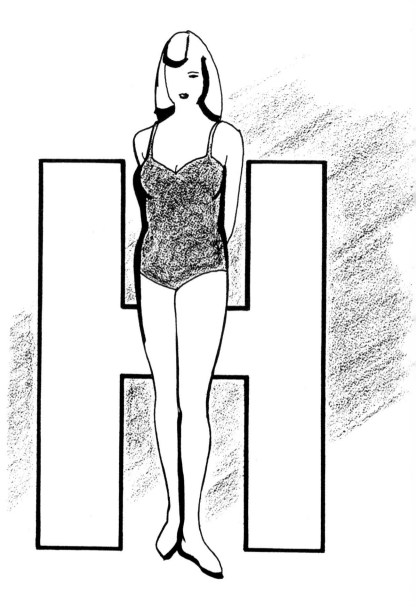

8-FRAME

1. This frame is curvy and perfectly balanced.

2. Bust is full and waist is small with average length.

3. Hips are gently tapered with good proportions to derriére.

4. Leg length and upper torso length are balanced.

5. Weight gain is always evenly distributed; Elizabeth Taylor is a good illustration of this figure's gain and loss.

Your goal with this figure is to emphasize the waist and avoid cluttering the figure with lots of clothes or layers. To do this you should choose garments that fit the body and identify the waist.

Figure Problems

By now, you should be able to determine the difference between your minor figure problems and your major ones, and you should be able to define your goal. If you found that you have some characteristics from more than one category, then you simply have a combination frame or a frame that is balanced. Just follow the recommendations for your figure problems and remember to create good balance from top to bottom.

If you are attempting to analyze your own figure, stand in front of a full length mirror and simply look for the obvious problems. Start with your neck — remember that the neck appears longer on sloping shoulders and shorter on square ones.

NECKS

If you visually have a long neck, you should not wear short hair, at least not short in the back. As you consider what necklines to wear, remember they frame your face and create a direction for the eye to follow. High necklines shorten the neck because they carry the eye upward.

Long necks should choose the following:
- high collars (mandarin, stand-up, and Cossack collars)
- turtlenecks
- cowl-necks
- accessories include chokers, necklaces, ribbons or scarves

Long necks should avoid:
- short hair and low necklines

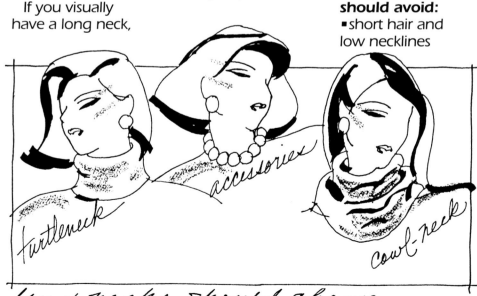

turtleneck

accessories

cowl-neck

long necks should choose . . .

Short necks should choose the following:
- open collars
- shawl collars
- V-necklines
- short hairstyles
(These lines bring the eye downward and lengthen the neck.)

Short necks should avoid the following:
- clutter around the neck
- any high neck styles

Another feature to consider is your "headset". Is it forward from the sideview of your body or is it even with it? If your headset is forward, then choose to wear your hair full in the back of the neck, as well as collars to disguise it nicely.

SHOULDERS

As you observed your neck, you may have already noticed whether your shoulders are sloping, square or have an average taper. Obviously, if you have sloping or narrow shoulders, you need shoulder pads. The type of pads you choose depends on the garment's sleeve style. If the sleeve is a set-in style, then you need a cut-off shoulder pad. This is currently the most popular style as the trend in fashion moves toward a softer, more natural look. However, regardless of what may be happening in fashion, shoulder pads will

V-neck   shawl collar   square

short necks should choose ...

always be a must for most mature women because they can take as much as 15 pounds and 15 years off your figure.

Narrow shoulders should choose the following:
- shallow/wide necklines such as boatnecks
- horizontal patterns on the shoulders
- set-in sleeves

- puffed sleeves
- detail on the shoulder edges
- cap sleeves
- fabrics that do not droop or cling to the shoulders
- wider lapels that point upward

Narrow shoulders should avoid the following:
- raglan sleeves
- dolman, batwing, kimono and peasant sleeves
- deep or narrow necklines

cap sleeve

shawl collar

puff sleeve

shoulder detail

horizontal on shoulder

lapel points upward

narrow shoulders should choose . . .

v-neck

no sleeve

kimona

raglan

narrow shoulders should avoid . . .

Broad shoulders should choose the following:

- dolman, batwing, kimono and peasant sleeves
- vertical stripes or tucks
- deep/ narrow necklines
- narrower lapels that point downward
- collars scaled to shoulder size for balance

If you have broad shoulders, you should still wear shoulder pads – thin shoulder pads. They detract from the shoulder and arm that is "fleshy" and full, and they cause the garment to hang nicely. Don't worry about having "football shoulders"— instead look at the positive results!

The average shoulder can wear almost any style sleeve, however, the raglan sleeve does cause the shoulder's appearance to drop forward. Shoulder pads can help correct this look.

BUST

The bustline should be firm and rounded in appearance. That should tell you immediately that a good fitting bra is crucial! (Next to a good hairstyle, a good bra is the most important feature involved in a good self-image.)

When I help a woman shop for the first time, we always begin in the foundations department because a good fitting bra can change the way her clothes fit.

Principle number one in fitting a bra is to find one that supports you without the straps being tightened.

broad shoulders should choose ...

Generally, this means an underwire style is needed. The straps are not to function like a harness that holds you in place; instead, their purpose is to smooth the cups. So, if you have red indentation marks under your bra straps, this indicates your bra is not supporting your breasts, but your straps are. Also, there should be no flesh bulging in front of the cups.

The second principle in fitting your bra is that it should hold your bustline no more than three inches below your armpit. Sports or natural bras do not flatter most women; they cause the breasts to swing out to the sides, flatten and drop. Obviously, their purpose is not for support.

If you are large busted, that is you wear a size D or larger, there are certain garment lines that will flatter your figure more than others. To avoid having to buy clothing that is one to two sizes larger than the rest of your body, choose a style that has a shoulder yoke with gathers or small pleats in the bodice of the garment.

Large busts should choose the following:
- V-necks
- small lapels or none at all
- shawl collars
- vertical or diagonal lines
- single small button fronts on softly tailored blouses

large bust should choose ...

details at bust

horizontal lines at bust

tight top-wide belt

ruffles

stiff fabric-pockets

large bust should avoid ...

Large busts should avoid the following:

- horizontal lines at the bust
- high-waisted looks
- stiff fabrics
- tube tops or anything tight
- patch breast pockets
- smocking at the bust
- large ruffles or bows at the bustline
- wide belts

Large breasted women should try to avoid looking matronly or top heavy. One flattering bodice line is the surplice wrap or "cross your heart" style. If you wear a DD or larger, then you should shop for a bra minimizer. This will give you good support and reduce the apparent size of your bust. It will definitely take pounds off and give your figure a more youthful appearance.

The small busted woman has more of an advantage in selecting clothing than the large busted one. She does not have the limitations as to what she can wear; her goal is to fill out the bustline.

Small busted women should choose the following:
- blousy designs
- layers of clothing
- pockets at the bust
- details in the bust area that express personal style
- padded bras (push up style will benefit your figure the most)

Small busted women should avoid the following:
- garments that are flat in bodice

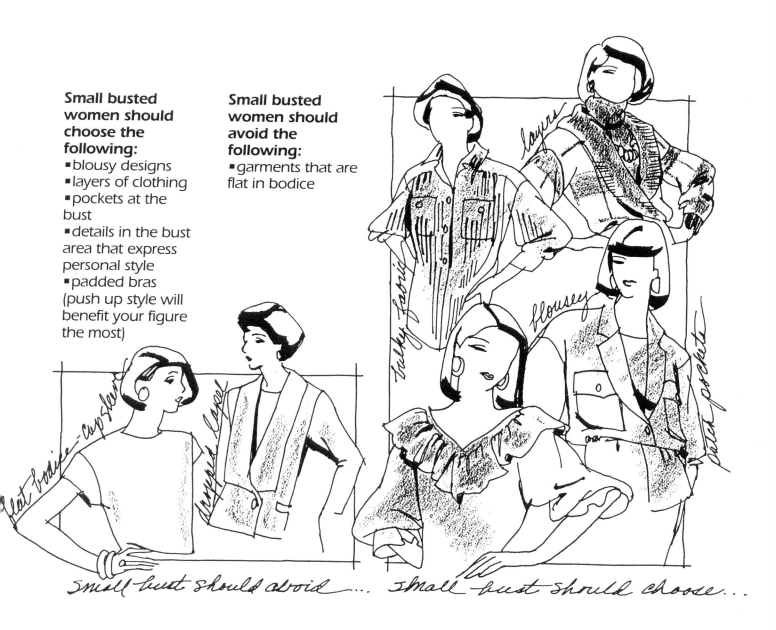

flat bodice - crop sleeve

dropped lapel

bulky fabric

layers

blousey

patch pockets

small bust should avoid ... Small bust should choose...

WAIST

The day of the small waist is long gone. Today's average waistline is 27 - 28 inches, with 25 inches considered to be small. If you have a tapered hip, then more than likely you have an average to long waistline that is small in comparison to the rest of your figure, and your rib cage is probably slender as well. You are the lucky one who can have lots of fun with belts of various widths. However, if you are thick waisted, don't assume you cannot wear belts. Everyone can wear them; they just wear them differently.

The thick waist is usually accompanied by a wider rib cage and a short to average waist length.

Thick-waisted women should choose the following:
- 1 1/2 inch belts (same color as the garment)
- belt buckle as a focal point
- slacks with pleats and pressed creases
- high or low waisted styles
- tunic tops
- overblouse
- Chanel-style jackets
- chemises
- loose vests or cardigan sweaters
- dropped blouson-style dresses
- one-piece bathing suits
- no contrast between top and bottom

Thick-waisted women should avoid the following:
- drawing attention to the entire waist
- contrast at the waistline

If you have a thick waist, your goal is to either disguise it altogether by hiding it under a straight garment or to create a small waist appearance by blousing above and below a belted look. Either can be done if you are not too overweight. Just remember, measurement is not important. Appearance is what you need to be concerned about.

If your pantyhose are too tight, too long or too short, they can distort your waistline. If they are too tight or if you need to roll the waist over to take up slack, you can simply clip the waist reinforcement to give more comfort. This technique works well with regular and light support hose. Ideally, you need to search for pantyhose that fit your proportions the best.

overblouse

long jacket

waist enter front focal point

chemise

dropped bosom

vest

ornate belt

thick waists should choose...

SHORT WAIST

Short-waisted figures find that one piece garments are too long in the waist. They also find that a belt with any width at all tends to take up all the space between their bust and waist. If this is your problem, then try wearing separates instead of one piece garments. When wearing a blouse with a skirt or pants, make sure you blouse the top over the waist to lengthen its appearance.

To visually determine if you are short waisted, drop your arm to your side with the palm of your hand facing forward. If the crease on the front side of your elbow lines up within one inch of your waist, you are average waisted. However, if your elbow crease falls more than one inch below the waist, you are on the short waisted side.

Short-waisted women should choose the following:
- narrow belts (no smaller than 1", no larger than 1 1/2")
- stiffened-back self-belts with buckles
- belts that match the top garment, not the bottom
- unfitted jackets
- overblouse
- longer open vests
- tunics (if tall enough)
- outfits of one color
- loose layers

Short-waisted women should avoid the following:
- wide waistbands
- wide belts (more than 1 1/2" wide)
- bare midriff
- tight-fitting tops
- short jackets
- horizontal lines on the bodice
- high-waisted pants or skirts
- contrasting colors at the waist

LONG WAIST

Long-waisted figures find that most one-piece garments are not long enough in the waist. To visually determine if you are long waisted, use the same procedure as for the short waist, but the elbow crease will fall

one color

loose layers

dropped waist

tunic

short waist should choose...

short jacket

wide belt

high waist

short waist should avoid...

yoke with horizontal stripe

belt matches bottom garment

wide tops

high waist

wide belt

long waist should choose....

more than one inch above the natural waistline.

Long-waisted women should choose the following:
- belts that match the bottom garment, not the top
- wide belts
- blouses tucked in, pulled out only when belted
- Empire styled waists
- tops with yokes
- tops with horizontal stripes or pockets

Long-waisted women should avoid the following:

- low rise pants
- dropped waist styles
- low slung belts
- overblouse
- blousons
- short hemlines, if also short legged
- narrow belts

HIPS

There are two hip problems; one is the high wide hip and the other is the low hip or saddlebag problem. Our goal with either is to disguise it! The wide high hip often has a thick

blouson... short cropped pants

low-slung belts

long overblouse

long top... short skirt

dropped waist

long-waisted should avoid...

shoulder pads

vertical lines down

modified dirndle

dropped waist - flared skirt

tunic top

wide hips should choose . . .

waist. The low hip usually has a slender rib cage with a nice waistline tapering gradually onto the hips. There are many figures that have a modification of both problems, and this can give a more balanced figure as long as the other areas of the body are not out of proportion.

Wide hips should choose the following:
- modified dirndl skirts (about three inches of ease into waistband)
- vertical lines from the waist down
- shoulder pads to balance hips
- pants with pressed creases
- belts worn slightly above the waist
- control-top pantyhose (takes five pounds off the figure)

Wide high hips should avoid the following:

- pockets at the hipline
- large plaids
- horizontal lines at the waist and hips
- narrow shoulder lines
- clingy/fitted tops
- wide belts
- full dirndl skirts
- straight box pleats
- wide-wale corduroy pants or skirts
- tight pants; clingy fabrics
- back pockets
- front/rear patch pockets

narrow top

horizontal at hips

full pocket

short crop top

pocket at hips

wide dirndl

large plaid pant

wide-wale corduroy

tight pants

wide hips should avoid...

Kangaroo top

long tweed jacket

long jacket

A-line

shoulder pads

swing coat

low hips should choose . . .

Low hips/ saddlebags should choose the following:

- A-line or flared skirts
- long vest or jackets
- moderately tapered or fitted jackets
- sleeves that are narrow at the wrist
- shoulder pads to balance the hips
- gentle swing coats (3/4's or longer)

**Low hips/
saddlebags
should avoid the
following:**
- pockets on the
hips
- excessive fullness
in skirts or pants
- pants that cup
under derriére
- pants or skirts
that are too tight
- horizontal lines
at hips
- pleated skirts
- bulky fabrics
- full gathered
skirts

cups under derriére

pleats & pockets on hips

too full skirt

horizontal lines at hips

pants too tight

skirt too tight

low hips should avoid.

from pants to face

overblouse

chemise

gored skirt

waistless dress

darts & soft pleats

Tummy problems should choose...

STOMACHS

Most women believe they have a tummy problem, however, a real tummy problem exists only if it protrudes beyond the bustline. Correct posture would cure that problem for many of us. There are many garment styles that disguise or minimize the tummy.

Tummy problems should choose the following:
- overblouse with a soft hang
- pants with a soft pleat and dart combination
- chemise-style dresses
- flared or gored skirts

- skirts with pleats that are sewn down
- flat strong fabrics
- waistless dresses
- focal point at the face
- pant zipper inside the left pocket

Tummy problems should avoid the following:

- full gathered skirts
- wide belts
- fly front on pants
- pleated skirts from the waist band
- straight, bouffant or gored skirts that cup under the tummy
- horizontal lines at the tummy
- clingy fabrics

skirt tucks under tummy

focal point at tummy

horizontal lines at tummy

fly front

wide belts

clingy fabrics

tummy problems should avoid ....

long jacket

long jacket...full skirt

back fullness

fullness not fanny

flat fannies should choose...

problem

FLAT FANNY

If your pants and straight skirts sag or bag in the "seat" area , then you have a flat fanny. Alterations in this area can often alleviate the sag, but ideally you should find those manufacturers who make pants and skirts to fit your shape. Your goal with this problem is to disguise it altogether or to create the illusion of more shape.

Flat fannies should choose the following:
- fullness to create shape off the waist on the backside.

- tapered jackets
- two-piece garments
- blouses worn belted on the outside of pants or skirts
- peplums
- box jackets with full skirts

Flat fannies should avoid the following:
- pants and skirts that sag or droop in the seat
- one-piece knits that cling
- pencil slim skirts

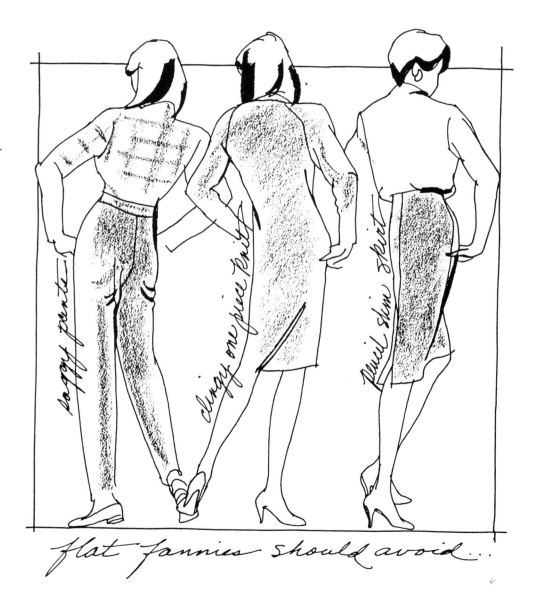

baggy pants

clingy one-piece knit

pencil slim skirt

flat fannies should avoid...

LEGS

Legs appear long or short depending on the length of the torso. A longer waist or torso will usually mean short legs are attached! Your goal is to balance the lower body with the upper body.

Short legs should choose the following:
- high heels (no more than 2 1/2 inches unless you are tall)
- high-waisted garments
- longer skirt hemlines

Short legs should avoid the following:
- cuffs on pants

longer skirt

top interest

high waist

short legs should choose....

cuff on pants

short legs should avoid...

Heavy legs should choose the following:

- straight or full leg pants
- pressed pant creases
- culotte skirts
- 2 - 3 inch heels
- matching skirt, hose and shoes
- styles with a focal point at the neck or shoulders
- darker bottoms and lighter or brighter tops

Heavy legs should avoid the following:

- dainty pumps
- strappy sandals
- thin, dainty shoes

light top

dark bottom

skirt match

shoes, hose &

split skirt

focal point at neck

strait leg-pressed joint

heavy legs should choose . . . .

long waists style

longer jacket

hem below the knee

cuffs on pants

tunic

strappy sandals

longer legs should choose ...

Longer legs should choose the following:
- long jackets, below the crotch
- tunics
- long-waisted styles
- cuffs on pants
- hems in straight skirts should fall just below the knee
- dainty pumps
- strappy sandals
- thin high heels

Long legs should avoid the following:
- dark hose
- clunky shoes
- skirts that are too long or too short
- high-waisted styles

ARMS

Whether you have thin or heavy arms, your goal is to disguise the size as much as possible.

Heavy arms should choose the following:
- loosely fitted sleeves
- wide arm cuts
- dolman or kimono sleeves are good if shoulder pads are used
- elbow length or long sleeves

Heavy arms should avoid the following:
- clingy fabrics
- tight sleeves
- sleeveless tops
- puffy, cap or short sleeves
- cuffs on sleeves

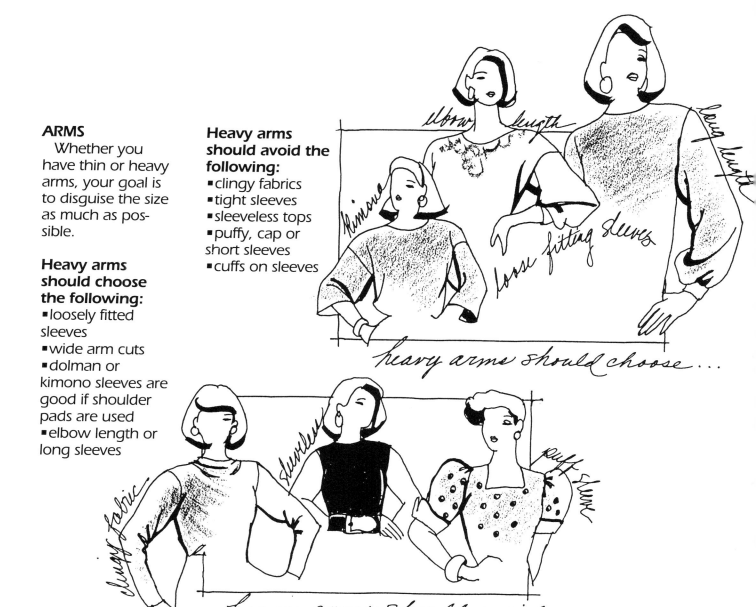

heavy arms should choose ...

heavy arms should avoid ...

loose fitting

wide above the elbow

bulky sleeve

Thin arms should choose . . .

Thin arms should avoid . . .

Thin arms should choose the following:
- sleeves that are wide and full above the elbow
- loose fitting sleeves
- bulky sleeves
- horizontal lines

Thin arms should avoid the following:
- tight sleeves
- tight turtleneck tops
- cap sleeves
- sleeveless or strapless tops

Once you learn to make the right choices for your garment lines, you will deceive the eyes of others all the time. No one will ever know what your figure problems really are. This will bring greater satisfaction and confidence to your image development. Remember, you need to learn the rules first; then you can try breaking some of them with success. Just make sure that you rely on the trained eye that you are developing as you decide what works best for you.

5
Getting Into the Swim of Things

To wear a swimsuit or not, that is the big question for so many women each and every spring or summer. We all have our reasons why we dread buying and wearing one. For some it is cellulite and saddlebags, for others it is fat knees, a tummy, a thick waist, too much or too little bust. Even if it's varicose veins, you can have injections that will cause them to disappear, although I have always thought someone should design a bathing suit with leggings. Wouldn't that be perfect?! I believe I hear some of you laughing!

The lighting in most store dressing rooms is enough to discourage you before you have even finished trying on the first suit. It is very common for a woman to try on two dozen suits and never buy one. If this is your plight, all you need to know is what to look for in a suit style.

The typical A-frame has a lower hip-saddlebag problem. For you, the "french cut" leg is good because it adds the leg length needed to slim your legs. If it is a two-piece, then choose the style that has the band at the waist. If you are long waisted, this will give you the helpful horizontal line to shorten your waist and the lycra fabric will help flatten the tummy. Ideally then, the top should have a wide V-neckline into the shoulder strap or a horizontal line at the bust or shoulder to add the needed width for balance to the hips. If a one-piece is preferred, the same leg cut and neckline will be best. For the small busted A-frame, a ruffled top or shaped cups with sheared fabric over it is a great enhancer.

Now if you are an H-frame with a straighter figure or are thick waisted, one piece styles will be best for you. Built-in bras are great for the full or small busted woman. For women who deal with the embarrassment of nipple exposure, there are small 2 1/2" to 3" pads that slip into the cups. They are available in some specialty shops or department stores.

A vertical line with sheared fabric down the left or right front of the suit will slim the figure. A V-front bodice design to below the waist will also slim the midriff area. If the fanny is flat, do not choose a European high cut leg, especially if the legs

French cut leg

French cut leg · waist contrast for long waist

Saddle bags should choose...

large bust ruffle at bottom

Small bust ruffle at top

V-front below waist

contrast at bust draws eye away from thick waist

large or Small bust
Should choose ...

thick waist should choose.

are longer than the upper body. The fanny needs more coverage to be more flattered. Less angle to leg cut will accomplish this. If you are slim and short-waisted, then the bikini will lengthen your torso.

The V-frame usually has two problems; a large, full bust and a flat fanny with a straighter waist line. A good bra top with a skirted style bottom would be best for needed balance. A surplice wrap style top will give a very flattering line to the bust.

Of course the curvy figure that is not heavy can do anything.

Shopping Tips

- When buying a bathing suit, choose one size larger than you normally wear in clothes. This gives you the needed length, not more width.
- Name brands are building in tummy controls into their lycra fabric suits.
- European cuts expose the "buns" and American cuts do not.

- Two-toned suits can be very flattering if the high color contrast is from the bust line upward. This draws the eye to the face.
- Beware of high contrast at the waist or hip line if you are thick-waisted or large hipped.
- Halter strap styles cannot be worn successfully on narrower sloping shoulders.
- Become familiar with specialty shops or talk to buyers for bathing suit departments to learn about the various cuts of the different manufacturers.

Color Tips

- Fair skins, regardless of season, do not wear black, white, navy, or extremely dark or light colors.
- Fair skins choose primary colors for the slimmer look.
- Dark skins look best in black, white or extremely dark or light colors.
- Warm/peachy skins should choose periwinkles, corals, apple greens, mustards or metallic golds for skin compliment.

6
Is Your Personality Showing?

Clothing personality is something everyone has, but many are not sure how best to express it. You may already know what yours is, but perhaps you haven't been able to pull it together into a total look or good personal style.

Personal style is an outward expression of an inner attitude about ourselves. It is the totality of our look—from hairstyle to shoes. It is evidenced by how we put our clothes together on our figure and finish it off with accessories. Someone with good personal style understands her colors, what lines and designs flatter her body, and how to express her personality through her clothing choices. She has cultivated and developed good taste and she puts it all together with harmony and consistency. She is a woman who always looks good, whether you see her at a party, the supermarket, on the job or happen to catch her in her bathrobe. Please, remember that personal style is a lifelong process. Each of us is at a different point in the process. So, don't stop reading because you are afraid this is too ambitious of an undertaking.

If you have a laid-back attitude, you will need to apply a greater effort in this venture than someone who has either an adventuresome spirit or a more perfectionist type of temperament. The following guidelines should help you:

1. You need to develop a new awareness of what "put together" women are doing.

2. Seek professional advice on your wardrobe building.

3. Observe the principles professionals use as they work with you.

4. Remember successful people are not intimidated

by what they don't know.

5. You Can Learn!

Your clothing personality is a very important part of your personal style. It is determined by your body structure, the type of hair and facial features you have, and by your lifestyle. Some people instinctively know what style or personality of clothes they like. Others, because of being impressionable or due to their desire to please others, may even have a style dictated to them. This often happens to the professional, especially if she has a very conservative employer. It happens to people in the entertainment business and political arena every day.

As I said, clothing personality is a very important part of good personal style; however, it is not the only part. The following features are also important components of good personal style:

1. Colors that compliment the natural hair, skin and eye colors.

2. Hair color that is correct for your skin tone.

3. Cosmetics that compliment the skin tone and enhance the eyes.

4. Clothing lines that compliment the figure frame and disguise any figure flaws.

5. Clothing that says, "This is who I am at my best!"

6. Accessories that harmonize with the lines and personality of the garment worn.

7. Fabrics that are compatible with each other.

8. Dressing consistently with your personality and lifestyle; wearing the greatest look for whatever activity you are involved in.

9. Keeping current with your look.

10. Maintaining a rich or quality look.

(It does not have to be expensive.)

To further clarify, I would like to add a list of less tangible qualities. These would describe the attitude of a woman who has achieved good personal style.

1. Ageless. She decides she will never become dowdy or matronly.

2. Mysterious. She has a certain element of fascination, not revealing-all about herself.

3. Sophistication. She is wise in the ways of the world, but doesn't follow them unless it's appropriate to do so.

4. Confident. She is comfortable with

her body and look, thus enabling her to concentrate on others without a nagging concern for how others see her.

Now, let's take a look at the categories of clothing personalities. There are six categories that are quite commonly used in reference to clothing styles. You may find that one suits you perfectly, or that you are a combination. Sometimes an influence of a third category enters the picture by way of fabric, pattern or accessories. As you consider which one(s) describe your look, or desired look, think carefully

about the essence of the personality before you choose it for yourself.

Basic Clothing Personalities

CLASSIC
The look is timeless, but fashionable. Your priority, to be well put together.

The Pitfalls: Becoming boring and predictable-too conservative.

DRAMATIC
The look may be high fashion, trendy or even mod. Your priority, to have and wear the "latest" look.

The Pitfalls: Becoming cheap,

tacky and lacking class.

ROMANTIC
The look is sexy, feminine, and curvaceous.

The Pitfalls: Becoming cheap or looking like a street walker, lacking class.

INGENUE
The look is innocent and feminine; not sexy.

The Pitfalls: Becoming quietus and outdated.

NATURAL
The look is sporty, casual and often country. Your priority, comfort first!

The Pitfalls: Developing a masculine image,

becoming outdated, looking too classic, or "Plain Jane".

GAMIN
The look is petite, sporty or miniature natural. Your priority, comfort first.

The Pitfalls: Developing a masculine image, becoming outdated, looking too classic, or "Plain Jane".

Combination Clothing Personalities
Combination personalities exist where the dominant personality is determined by physical structure/ body type, hair type and style

preferences along with facial features. The secondary personality is determined by lifestyle and some personal preferences.

Examples and Workable Combinations:

Classic/Dramatic is predominately Classic because of physical appearance but also may be Dramatic because of professional involvement and personal preference for the unusual in accessories. Other Classic combinations are **Classic**/Romantic, **Classic**/Natural, **Classic**/Gamin.

Dramatic/Classic is predominately Dramatic because she is tall and slender with unusual facial features and severe hairstyle. Her job may dictate that her dress be more Classic. However, she will always choose to add some unusual flares to her look and in her casual dress she'll be very trendy or artsy. Other Dramatic combinations are **Dramatic**/Romantic, **Dramatic**/Natural.

Romantic/Classic is predominately Romantic because of her curvy figure and feminine features. Her job may require her to be professionally Classic in her dress. Feminine features might appear as a bit of lace on a collar or in a floral blouse of soft fabric. Another Romantic combination is **Romantic**/Dramatic.

Ingenue/Natural is predominately the Ingenue which is determined by her youthful, feminine figure and facial features with soft curly hair. If her job dictates, she will choose to wear some sportier clothes for practicality's sake. Other Ingenue combinations are **Ingenue**/Gamin, **Ingenue**/Classic.

Natural/Classic is predominately Natural because of her sturdy body build, facial features and easy care hairstyle. Her job may dictate more Classic clothing for daywear. In her casual wear, you will always find her in a pair of jeans or comfortable sweats. Other Natural combinations are **Natural**/Dramatic, **Natural**/Ingenue, **Natural**/Gamin.

Gamin/Classic personality is determined by her petite but sturdy frame, facial features and easy care hairstyle. She may choose very Classic/Professional suits or dresses for work wear. In her leisure, she will go right to her jeans or sweats for comfort. Other Gamin combinations are **Gamin**/Ingenue, **Gamin**/Natural.

Classic Evening . . .

THE CLASSIC

The Classic can be the epitome of elegance. One seasonal color palette especially lends itself to this quality, Summer. Some color/image systems would say that if you are a Summer, then you are a Classic. However, I believe that any season can be any personality, especially since most women are combination personalities. When we look at body type, facial features, hairstyle and clothing preferences of this person, it is not difficult to understand why any season can be a Classic.

Body Type
1. Average height and build

2. Balanced figure, mature appearance

3. Not too thin, delicate or sturdy

4. Silhouette is often softly straight

Clothing
1. Conservative but fashionable

2. Refined and ladylike

3. Dignified and sophisticated

4. Not trendy, faddish or severe

5. Lines may be soft or softly flared

6. No crisp or bouffant lines

NOTE: Her goal is to be well put together.

Face
1. Average to attractive

2. Regular features

Hairstyle
1. Good cut

2. Controlled style

Accessories
1. Refined, elegant and fashionable

2. Fine or good costume jewelry

3. Shoes: classic pump or sling backs

4. Scarves: silks to challis

Classic Casual ...

Classic Business & Daywear ...

Natural

Angenue

Classic
Combinations . . .

Dramatic

Fabrics

1. Low-luster preferred over high-luster

2. Refined textures: silks, gabardines, crepes, challis, chiffon, cottons and cashmere

3. Solid colors preferred

4. Patterns or prints are conservative

5. Rounded figures: best in florals or polka dots

6. Straighter figures: best in stripes, solids, abstracts or houndstooth check

Prototypes

Grace Kelly, Nancy Reagan, Candice Bergen, Barbara Walters, Linda Evans, Dina Merrill, Margaret Thatcher

THE DRAMATIC

The Dramatic is expressed in either a sophisticated, high fashion look or an artsy look. The latter can be extreme and outrageous with her image. You will immediately visualize this if you think of Cher. The more sophisticated high fashion image is usually richer in appearance, allowing it to move into some business or professional settings more easily than the artsy one. Wherever she goes, the Dramatic causes heads to turn. People want to see what she has on and how she has put it all together.

The Winter is the most obvious and typical Dramatic because the colors are so vivid and can be highly contrasted. The Autumn can create drama with her rich colors also. The Summer and Spring are rarely 100% dramatic because they can't create the drama with their softer colors, so they will be a combination with one of the other types.

Body Type
1. Tall, slender, and exotic is typical

2. May be short and slender

3. Could be average to tall and heavy

Clothing
1. May be high fashion and sophisticated

2. May be artsy, trendy or avant-garde

3. Daywear: high fashion or extremely plain garments, chic and contemporary

4. Evening: exotic, ethnic or costume

5. Lines: severe or bouffant

Note: Her goal is to have the latest look.

Dramatic Business & Daywear ...

Dramatic Casual . . .   *Dramatic Evening* . . .

Face

1. Prominent features: sharply angular or defined

2. High cheekbones, pointed chin, striking eyes (when made-up)

3. Make-up: dramatic or extreme

Hairstyle

1. Severe styles best: asymmetrical cuts, very long, braids, or chignon

2. Color: typically dark on a true dramatic

Accessories

1. Jewelry: bold, contemporary, ethnic, sometimes very ornate

2. Belts: large and ornate

3. Scarves: large silks or challis shawls

4. Hats: very unusual and dramatic

Fabrics

1. Solids or patterns: bold in color

2. Patterns: abstract, geometric or ethnic

3. Evening: shiny, glittery, ornate

Prototypes

Tina Turner, Diana Ross, Lauren Bacall, Shari Belefonte Harper, Barbra Streisand, Marlene Dietrich

Dramatic Combinations...

Romantic Casual...

THE ROMANTIC

The Romantic is a sexy "lady", born to be curvy and very feminine. She is the epitome of femininity and sex appeal as a mature adult. This woman does not have plastic surgery to create a full bust, rounded hips and small waistline; her attributes are God-given. Obviously, she needs to dress in keeping with her femininity, but with good taste and appropriateness, or she will look like a street-walker. When she enters a room full of people, most of the women will feel threatened by her appearance.

Body Type
1. Average to short, usually not tall

2. Rounded feminine figure, hourglass shape

3. Proportions: balanced, no flaws

4. If overweight, figure is still romantic and evenly balanced

Clothing
1. Dresses preferred: body shaping or waist revealing

2. Sweater girl: Angora or cashmere

3. Suits: if worn are lightly tailored with silky, feminine blouses

NOTE: Her goal is to look very feminine.

Romantic Business & Daywear . . .

Romantic Evening . . .

Dramatic

Classic

Romantic Combinations...

Face
1. Soft, rounded features

2. Large, flirty eyes

3. Natural feminine beauty

4. Rich coloring in whatever season

Hairstyle
1. Curls and curves best if hair is long

2. Feathered cut best if hair is short

3. Soft and bouncy

4. Never straight or stringy

Accessories
1. Jewelry: dainty in detail and lavish in effect, diamonds or rhinestones

2. Scarves: silk florals

3. Silk or real flowers

Fabrics
1. Medium to lightweight

2. Silk, crepe, knits, Angora, cashmere

3. Evening: velvet, lace, chiffon, satin

4. Patterns: soft blended or contrasted florals or polka dots

Prototypes
Liz Taylor, The Gabor Sisters, Jaclyn Smith, Marilyn Monroe, Lynda Carter, Joan Collins, Ann-Margret, Marie Osmond, Jane Seymore

THE INGENUE

The Ingenue differs from the Romantic in that she is the innocent personality. She is not sexy and alluring, but instead has a fresh, youthful quality. All Romantics are Ingenues as small children, and at some point in their growth, they mature into Romantics. The similarity in both personalities is their natural femininity. Some women are Ingenues all their lives. Helen Hayes is a perfect example of one. When an Ingenue enters the room, she brings a quality of freshness. She is not threatening.

Remember this quality when you decide between a Romantic and an Ingenue.

Body Type
1. Small-boned, not necessarily petite

2. Dainty, often delicate appearing

3. Naturally feminine

4. Gentle, rounded figure

Clothing
1. Dresses preferred

2. Eyelet trimmed, ruffles, tucks and lace

3. "Old fashioned" feminine styles

Ingenue Casual...

Ingenue Evening...

Ingenue Business & Daywear...

4. Simple clothes in feminine fabrics

5. Manufacturers: Laura Ashley, Susan Briston, etc.

Note: Her goal is to look feminine, but innocent.

Face

1. Rounded cheeks and chin

2. Fine boned

3. Large innocent eyes

3. Delicate coloring in whatever season

Hairstyle

1. Softly curled when long or short

2. Feather cut if short

3. Soft bounce

Accessories

1. Jewelry: Small and dainty

2. Floral ceramics, cameos, ribbons

3. Bows in hair or on clothes or shoes

Fabrics

1. Lightweight: soft woolens, Angora, cashmere, fine silk, fine cottons, voille, gauze or knits

2. Evening: chiffon, organza, eyelet, open or crocheted knits

Prototypes:

Debbie Reynolds, Helen Hayes, Goldie Hawn, Charlene Tilton, Sandra Dee, Sally Struthers

Ingenue Combinations...

Natural ...

Business & Daywear ...

THE NATURAL

The Natural prefers comfort in her clothes, whether they be casual or dressy. Dressing-up is often an effort for her because of her preference for informality. One of the pitfalls when she dresses up is that she has a tendency to become Classic and looses the essence of her personality. She does this, for example, by choosing fabrics for dressy blouses in polyester, crepe de chine or charmeuse which are Classic. She should stay in cottons, rayon or silk broadcloth for dressy styles. I find that when it comes to choosing evening clothes, she really is at a loss. Unfortunately, the fashion industry caters to the Romantic or the Dramatic when it comes to evening clothes, which only complicates her dilemma. The Natural needs to stay with simple elegance for evening.

Body Type
1. Average to tall

2. Strong sturdy body

3. Average to broad shoulders

4. Athletic appearance

5. Wholesome, natural, outdoor type

Clothing
1. Sportswear (casual to chic)

2. Daywear: tailored separates preferred

3. Businesswear: tailored suits

4. Some like town and country look

5. Some like preppy, country club look (polo shirts, monograms, espadrilles)

6. Avoid frills and fuss

NOTE: Her goal is to be comfortable and look good but with little effort.

Face
1. Broad or long with square jaw

2. Natural look in makeup

3. Some are tanned and freckled

4. Friendly, smiling eyes are common

Hairstyle
1. Windblown and casual

2. Short to long

3. Unset and never fussy

4. May be naturally curly

Accessories
1. Prefers simplicity, finds this area difficult; often chooses size that's too small for body proportions

Natural Evening ...

Natural Casual . . .

2. Jewelry: chunky, natural woods or stones, some ethnic styles like Indian; some contemporary styles in costume jewelry

3. Scarves: Not preferred or comfortable, shawls are appropriate at times

4. Shoes: athletic shoes, flats, loafers, low-heeled pumps

Fabrics
1. Daywear: nubby textures, tweeds, raw silk, linen, corduroy, woolens, cottons

2. Patterns: plaids, checks, abstracts, and paisleys

3. Eveningwear: beautiful brocades, georgettes, crepes and velveteen

Prototypes:
Carol Burnett, Julie Andrews, Farrah Fawcett, Cheryl Tiegs, Ethel Kennedy

THE GAMIN

The Gamin is simply a scaled-down or petite Natural. They have the same priorities and preferences in clothing, etc. There is often a perkiness about their personality and a youthfulness about their figure and overall look. The Natural, on the other hand, has a more mature body.

Body Type

1. Small to medium build

2. Well coordinated

Gamin Business & Daywear ...

Gamin Casual ...

3. May be slender but is never fragile

4. Sturdy, but not large in stature

Clothing
1. Casual, snappy, chic

2. Small-scaled details

3. Avoid frills

4. Daywear: same as Natural

5. Eveningwear: same as Natural

Face
1. Small, rounded cheeks and chin

2. Square jawline

3. Often has turned up nose

4. Friendly face

5. Natural make-up

Hairstyle
1. Short or long

2. Straight or curly

3. Natural, wind-blown, casual

Accessories
1. Minimum amount

2. Jewelry: light-weight chains, simple rings, quality pins

3. Scarves: not preferred or comfortable

4. Shoes: athletic shoes, flats, loafers, lower heels are preferred

Fabrics

1. Casual: snappy and chic cotton weaves or knits, small pinwale corduroy

2. Daywear: soft tweeds, woolens, raw silk, linens, silk shantung, voilles, pique and novelty sheers

3. Patterns: small-scaled checks, plaids, stripes, small geometric prints, plaids and stylized florals like paisleys

4. Eveningwear: understated elegance in same type fabrics as Natural

Prototypes:
Natalie Wood, Sandy Duncan, Karen Valentine, Bonnie Franklin, Sally Field, Mary Lou Retton

Gamin Combinations ...

7
Accessorizing: Pulling Your Look Together

It has been said that, "Accessories are the leading symbols of a woman's true personality." If this is true, then each of us should start our image development by taking inventory of our accessories. Accessories are anything that is worn except the garment itself. This means that even your nail color is an accessory. Now, for some of you this inventory would take about 15 minutes, but others would need to spend three to four hours, maybe more! At any rate, our accessories are an expression of our personal style and personality.

Let's look at some of the functions of accessories, and then at the guidelines that are important as we apply them to our garments.

Accessory Functions

1. They make an outfit look complete or finished. This is definitely a confidence builder.

2. They give visual appeal to plain lines and neutral colors.

3. They create the mood of the outfit if it does not already have one "built-in."

4. They can change the mood of any outfit.

5. They can give a variety of looks to a single outfit.

Accessory Guidelines

1. They should be an expression of your own personal style or clothing personality.

2. They should feel and look right on you. This means you must feel comfortable wearing them, and their size and proportion should be scaled to your body and clothing.

3. They should be colors from your personal color palette.

4. They should be complimentary to the color of your outfit.

5. They should draw attention away from any problem areas. For example, if you have a hip problem, flashy bracelets are only going to draw attention to this area. Long necklaces draw attention away from the chin and neck, but draw attention to the bustline. Small chain necklaces make the shoulders appear broader, etc.

6. They should create only one focal point. This means as you look at yourself in the mirror, your eyes should be drawn to only one area, not bounce from one to another.

7. Your accessory (accent) color should be repeated at least once, two or three times maximum.

8. Never mix dressy garments with casual accessories, and vice-versa.

9. Some garments make a statement in themselves and they need very few accessories.

Having considered the functions and guidelines for accessorizing, let's consider the first area of application.

Shoes

1. The taller you are, the higher heel you can wear. If you are 5'3" or shorter, do not wear heels higher than 2 - $2\frac{1}{2}$ inches. Otherwise, you will look like you are walking on your tip-toes.

2. Your shoes should be the same color value as your hemline or darker. The exception is in casual wear. If in doubt, wear a neutral color.

3. When putting together an outfit, start with the shoes. The reason for this is that the clothing and the leather industries have not collaborated in their selection of colors. For example, you may find that navy in the leathers will be the Summer or Autumn shades, but the garment may be

the Winter shade. This obviously creates some difficulty in your coordination attempts. It is a good idea to buy two pairs of shoes to finish an outfit.

4. The classic pump is the most versatile dress shoe. It may have closed or open toes, or be sling-back.

5. If you have large legs, avoid straps across the instep of the foot or ankle, wider heels, and round or square toes. These styles enlarge legs and widen the foot.

6. Strappy high-heeled shoes are usually dressy and feminine. They are not appropriate with suits or tailored dresses.

7. Stacked heels with closed toes are strictly sporty and they do not go with dressy clothes.

8. Clunky shoes are not flattering to any leg size.

Shoe Leathers

Calf-skin: A standard shoe leather that is good year-round. It is appropriate for daytime, sport or casual. The heavier the leather, the sportier it is.

Kid-skin: This is good for day or evening, especially for dresses in light-weight fabrics.

Suede: This is good for day to evening, casual or dressy, fall or winter (it needs weighty fabrics). When worn in the spring, it must be with gabardine or challis because of its need for weighty fabrics. When suede shoes are worn, accessories must be suede also. It is the least durable of all leathers because it is fragile and sensitive. When driving a car, it is wise to wear a different pair of shoes to protect the heels from a worn look.

Patent: This is good for daytime, and is best for spring through fall. It can be worn year-round in warm climates. It is appropriate with lightweight fabrics like silks, linens, rayons or cottons. It is not considered an evening shoe unless it's worn in a slipper-style; then, it can also be worn all year.

Fabric: High-lustre fabrics, like satin, jeweled, or faille shoes, are appropriate for after-five. The low-lustre fabrics, like canvas, are for day-wear.

Reptile: Snake and eel skin shoes are good for elegant daytime wear, dress or casual chic. The snake skin can move into evening if desired.

Business:
- pumps
- spectators
- slingbacks
- T-straps

Casual:
- loafers
- flat sandals
- espadrilles
- huaraches
- sneakers
- moccasins
- Western boots
- clogs or slides

Dressy:
- strappy heels
- silk or brocade
- metallic
- Lucite
- jeweled

NOTE: Generally low-lustre metallics like pewter or bronze are for dressy daytime to casual looks, and the high-lustre metallics are for evening. The exception is the silver or gold flat shoes that can be worn with casual-chic clothing.

Hosiery

1. Hosiery is the finishing touch, not a focal point.

2. Hosiery needs to be in the same color base as the garment worn. Avoid warm hosiery colors with cool colors in clothing.

3. Colored hosiery may either match the garment or the accessory/accent color. If the hose match the color of the dress or skirt, they add the illusion of height and slimness, particularly in the basic or neutral colors.

4. If the hosiery color matches the accessory/accent color, it should not outshine the garment color.

5. If textured hose are desired, then the texture must balance with the texture of the fabric worn; light weight texture belongs with delicate fabric and heavy texture with heavy fabrics.

6. The best fitting hose come in the tube-style.

7. The most durable hose are the control-top, in any brand.

8. Lycra increases the durability of any type hosiery.

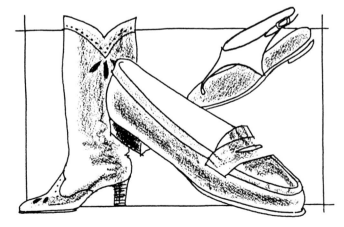

Handbags

1. They should always be "tried on".

2. The personality of the handbag should be compatible with the clothes worn — sporty with sporty; romantic with romantic, etc.

3. It should be the same color value as the shoes worn or lighter, and it should harmonize with the outfit colors.

4. The size of the handbag should fit between the pelvic bones when held against the front of the body.

5. The shoulder bag should never fall at the widest part of the hips, but at a narrower point above. Shoulder bags belong with pants or a tailored straight-line suit, otherwise, tuck the strap inside the purse.

6. Tapestry handbags are for casual use, not dressy. They are usually trimmed with natural leather or wood.

Belts

Belts add a great finishing look and can be worn with almost any outfit. No wardrobe is complete without a wide selection of

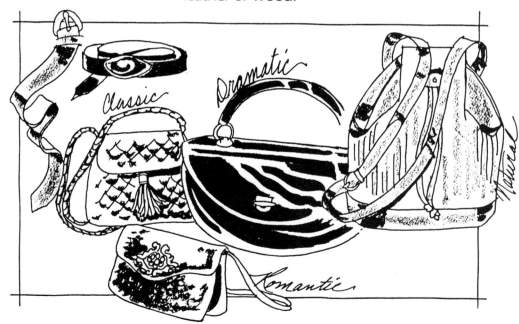

belts. Everyone can wear them, but we can't all wear them in the same way. You must remember the principles of good proportions.

1. The best belt buckles in the middle hole.

2. Square, rectangle or geometrics buckles are best with tailored garments.

3. The smooth, curved, oval or shell buckles complement the soft, curved body and detail lines.

4. The safest width is 1 1/2 inches.

5. The color, leather and style must be compatible with the other leather accessories.

6. Cinch belts should be worn only by small to average busts, not large.

7. Check your discount stores for good buys on better leather belts.

8. Large hips should never wear narrow or skinny belts. The width should be at least 1 inch and they should have a narrow buckle for a focal point. This creates the illusions of a smaller waist.

NOTE: A good basic belt NEVER goes out of style.

Scarves

Scarves are great items to finish a look. They may frame the face and neck, adorn the waist, or wrap the head and they never go out of style. They have become increasingly popular because accessories are a bigger item on the fashion scene than ever before. Because clothing is so expensive, scarves and other accessories that can change the look of a garment are a great alternative to buying a new outfit.

1. Scarves can pull contrasting color separates together.

2. Silk scarves are printed in florals, stripes, polka dots, geometrics or abstracts.

3. Florals are best with dresses or blouses that are feminine in personality.

4. Stripes, geometrics or abstracts are best with tailored clothes that are classic, dramatic or natural in personality.

5. Wool challis scarves are worn primarily with wools or weighty fabrics.

6. The way the scarf is tied should be compatible with the personality of the individual outfit.

Jewelry

Remember, there is a fine line between classy and brassy, meaning that you can overdo it with jewelry. Most women, however, do not use enough jewelry. The reason is that most are not sure what to do with it; the following principles will help.

NOTE: Always apply your perfume before putting on your jewelry to prevent damaging it.

1. The size of jewelry worn should be scaled to the bone structure of the face and body. A large woman should wear large jewelry because dainty jewelry tends to look lost. REMEMBER THE PRINCIPLES OF BALANCE.

2. Oversized garments call for oversized jewelry. This is seen in the dramatic style especially.

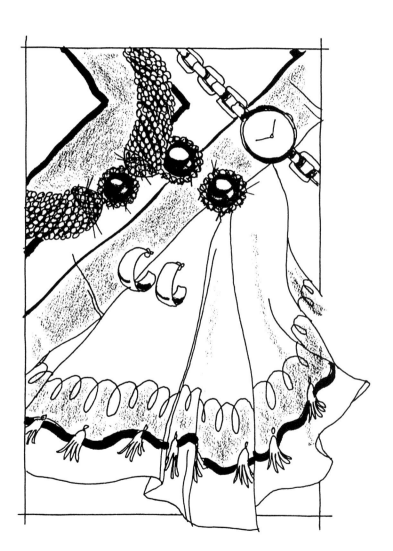

3. Jewelry application begins with the face first, neck second, and wrist third. A scarf may be substituted for a necklace or used in conjunction with it.

4. Brushed fine metals are dressier than highly polished ones.

5. Jewelry metal colors may be mixed. For example: silver with gold. They can look elegant on pastels or dazzling on darks.

6. The style of jewelry must suit the style and personality of the garment. Pearls, for instance, can be very classic or they can create a feminine, Victorian or romantic look, depending on the styling and the mix-with-metal design.

7. Sporty clothing and heavier textures require either simple or chunky natural jewelry. Romantic, feminine clothing requires feminine, more delicate accessories, as in fine jewelry.

8. If wearing a pin and a necklace together, you must wear the pin on a jacket or outside layer and the necklace on the dress or blouse.

9. You can wear clusters of pins on lapels. These pins could be earrings, which can also be used as shoe clips and scarf pins.

10. Jewelry pieces do not have to match but they should blend nicely.

11. Any piece of jewelry should be a perfect partner to several garments in your closet.

Hats

Even though very few women wear hats today, the fashion industry has not given up designing and manufacturing them. They add a wonderful dimension to many looks and certainly add a mysterious quality when worn correctly. It is usually the Dramatic or maybe the Romantic who wears them for a fashion statement. Classics are too concerned about damaging their hairstyle and the Natural does not usually even think of wearing one unless it would be for functional purposes.

Hats never go out of style, although they may be more in-style at some time than others. Like anything else, hat styles come and go. So make sure the hat stuck away in your closet is not out of style before you wear it. The following principles should be considered when choosing a particular hat to wear or purchase.

1. The brim of the hat should be no wider than the shoulders. The taller you are the bigger hat you can wear.

2. The crown of the hat should equal the width of your temples.

3. Most hats should be worn forward on the top of the head with the crown opening covering a portion of the forehead. Many of them should also be tilted on a slight angle. This is the only way a hat can be fashionable.

4. Straw hats go with light-weight fabrics like cottons, chiffons, linens, etc. Seasonally, they are worn in the spring or summer.

5. Flannels and felts go with wools or suedes. Seasonally, they are worn in the fall and winter.

6. If the hat and clothes are the same color, the hat must have a great shape or the clothes must be sharp and fashionable, otherwise the look will be boring.

7. With dark colors, choose a bright contrasting trim on the hat and pick this up as your accent color.

8. With pastel colors in clothes, choose a pastel in your hat selection that matches an accent color in another shade. Of course, you need to pick up this accent color in your other accessories.

9. Make sure the hat you choose compliments your face, face shape and profile.

Personalities of Hats

Sporty/Natural
- Felt fedora
- Beret
- Boater (gondolier)
- Large, textured straw hats
- Simple cloche
- Deerstalker (Sherlock Holmes)
- Cowboy hat
- Fisherman's hat

Classic
- Pillbox
- Wide-brimmed fedora
- Picture hats

Dramatic
- Anything unusual or extreme in style
- Deep cloche
- Turban
- Wide, deep pillbox
- Flat crown and brim
- Skull-cap with stiffened net brim and bow

Romantic
- Soft, floppy brimmed hats
- Pillbox with flowers
- Skull-cap with flowers
- Anything with flowers, bows or sparkles.

8

Is Fabric Compatibility Important?

There are three areas in which appropriate fabrics and their compatibility are important in creating a "total" look. They are as follows:

1. The texture and weight of the fabric must compliment your figure-type and personal style.

2. The fabrics of each garment piece in your outfit should be compatible to one another.

3. The fabrics in your accessories such as scarves, shoes, hairbows, etc., should be compatible with other garment fabrics you are wearing.

Fabric Texture and Weight

Whether you are at an average weight or 30 pounds overweight, if you have a curvy figure, fabrics that are crisps or stiff, man-tailored in appearance, or heavily textured, will not compliment your curves. They will only enlarge your appearance and destroy your natural femininity. Your best fabrics are soft; they drape well and are not too bulky. These include silks, soft wool crepes, jerseys, rayon crepes, challis and cotton knits or soft weaves.

Straight figures are most complimented by flat, crisp man-tailored fabrics like wool gabardine, shark skin, linen, and crisp cottons like poplin and trigger cloth. The figures which are softly curved or softly straight look best in fabrics which are neither too crisp or too drapey. These people have more flexibility in their choices than either of the other extremes.

The patterns or prints on the various fabric weights and weaves should also be considered. These can either compliment the body or destroy the desired look.

Generally speaking, geometric prints are best on crisp fabrics with tailored lines, whereas floral prints are best on soft fabrics with curved, feminine lines. Abstract patterns may have a soft appearance, a sharp dramatic look, or various ethnic expressions. This is where clothing style and personality interplays with fabric and line.

Garment Choices and Fabric Compatibility

As you consider your new clothing purchases, 50% of them should be in fabrics that are wearable the year round. This consideration includes the climate factor as well as fashionableness. The following fabrics would accommodate both cold and warm temperatures:

- Raw silk - dress, jumpsuit, suit, coat, pants
- Silk crepe de chine, broadcloth or tissue faille - dresses, blouses, scarves
- Cotton knits or sweaters - casual to semi-casual
- Wool or rayon gabardine - daywear for business
- Rayon silk blends - daywear for business
- Rayon crepe - daywear

The number one "cardinal" rule with fabric mixes is, "Never combine casual fabrics with dressy fabrics." A good example would be never mix a soft cotton knit dress with a linen-textured silk jacket. The dress is too casual a fabric for the dressier jacket. Many times a good clue will be the dressiness of the style in one versus the casualness of the other. Another good example is the inappropriateness of a washable silk blouse with a cotton poplin pant or skirt.

Retail clerks in the better stores can often be of help, but don't always depend on them. In many of the youth-oriented stores, they mix anything — good taste or not. Many times they seek to make an extreme statement rather than a good fashion statement. This is where you see dressy nylon lace combined with a casual crinkle cotton, etc. It is perfectly acceptable by young peers in schools and on campuses, but not in the more serious, business/social environments. When young people grow up wearing that type of look, they have a more difficult time choosing the "right" clothes when they get out in the business world.

The John T. Malloy image is certainly no longer the norm in the business world, especially not in the 90's. There is definitely more emphasis on personal style and good taste than on asexual business images.

Coming back more specifically to fabric compatibility, blouse fabrics that mix well with wool and wool blends are silks, cotton blends, polyester or a blend such as silk and wool. Blouse fabrics that mix well with linen, raw silks or cottons include lightweight linen or ramie, rayon, cotton and some silks or silk looks in polyester. Keep the weights and lustres balanced in mixing your fabrics, whether the same or contrasting.

Wintertime suit fabrics include the various wool weaves (flannels, tweeds, crepes or gabardines) and also wool blends.

Summertime suit fabrics include lightweight wool gabardine, linen or linen looks, rayon weaves, raw silk, silk linen and polyester blends. You will note that almost all summertime suit fabrics have some degree of texture, from very nubby to crisper linen textures.

Fabrics most suitable for wintertime dresses include wools (knits or weaves such as gabardine crepes or challis) and blends. These provide good choices for daywear or business looks. For evening and holiday wear, velvet, taffeta, chiffon, satin or brocade are good alternatives.

Fabrics most suitable for summertime dresses are the cottons, such as chambray, gauze, denim, broadcloth, (polished) sateen, knit, jacquard, eyelet or lace. Rayon challis, faille, and crepe are among some of the dressier fabrics along with silk.

For evening, chiffon, lace, eyelet or polished cotton are good choices.

When preparing to purchase any garment, the following questions should be considered:

1. Is the fabric casual or dressy?

2. Does the garment fabric present a quality image?

3. Does this fabric destroy the richness of its companion garment?

4. Are there too many textures or patterns among the garments to make them well-mated?

5. If it doesn't look right to your eye, then it probably is not. WHEN IN DOUBT, DON'T!

6. Is this garment/fabric suitable for my needs?

7. Can it be worn for several different occasions?

8. Will this fabric wear well?

9. Does this fabric wrinkle easily? Do I care?

10. Will the fabric texture in the garment work with other garments in my wardrobe?

At this point in our discussion of fabric, it is important to understand some of the characteristics of natural versus synthetic fabrics.

Assets of Natural Fibers (cotton, wool, silk, linen)
- Absorbs moisture nicely
- Are long-wearing
- Molds nicely into desired design; tailors beautifully
- Many have elegant feel or touch
- Can be altered, seams let out, without noticeable changes or pin-holes

Liabilities of Natural Fibers
- Drys slowly
- Soils easily
- Will shrink if not properly laundered or cleaned
- Permanent pressing is not possible by heat setting

Assets of Synthetic Fibers
- Blends well with natural fibers
- Doesn't shrink
- Requires little or no pressing
- Can be permanently pleated
- Produced in quantities at lesser cost
- Wrinkle resistant

Liabilities of Synthetic Fibers

- Stains easily
- Feels clammy in hot weather and cold in winter weather because they don't breathe or allow air circulation
- Collects static electricity
- Lacks durability
- Susceptible to grease stains
- Generally does not dye in clear, bright, intense colors well
- Usually retains perspiration odors

Rayon is not a natural fiber, but it has some qualities of a natural fiber such as breathability and comfort. Derived from a cellulose fiber, it does not have a chemical base.

Accessory Fabric and Clothes

Whenever you choose to use accessories made of fabric, compatibility is important. Some of the rules of past decades no longer apply to accessorizing your clothes today. For example, satin shoes were considered to be for evening-wear and wedding parties only. Now, they are being shown for day-wear in spring and summer. Sequin and rhinestone-trimmed garments used to be appropriate for evening-wear only; now we wear them for fun, casual/chic clothes during the day.

The general principles of day-wear/business clothing have not changed much, however. For instance, silk scarves are dressy and belong with this look. The dressier challis scarves are also compatible with dressy daywear garments. Casual cottons or rayon scarves belong with casual cottons and rayon garments.

Canvas shoes belong with casual cotton weaves or knits, not dressy clothes. The same is true with any other casual fabric shoe.

Fabric Definitions

Broadcloth: A lightweight plain weave, tightly woven in a thin yarn. As a cotton blend, it has a lustrous surface. Cotton or silk broadcloth is great for blouses and dresses.

Challis: A fine, lightweight fabric in smooth, firm weave. Challis is usually printed with a floral or paisley pattern. It drapes well for dresses, skirts and scarves.

Chambray: A lightweight weave of colored and white yarns for a cool look. Sometimes referred to as lightweight denim.

Charmeuse: A medium-weight satin fabric with high luster. It has a soft draping quality. Charmeuse is good for blouses and some dresses for dressy day-wear.

Cotton sheeting: This tightly woven, lightweight fabric has all the best qualities of cotton (coolness, crispness, breathability) and is also particularly durable.

Crepe: A soft, drapey fabric characterized by a slightly pebbly texture. Lighter weight is used for dresses, medium weight is used for dressy separates. Crepes may be silk, wool or rayon.

Crepe de chine: A very soft, lightweight fabric with a surface sheen and a silky feel. It creates a dressy look for blouses and dresses.

Denim: This rugged, durable fabric is available in the traditional indigo blue, plus gray and black. The heavier the weight, the more durable the fabric. Basically for casual wear.

Faille: A semi-lustrous fabric with ribbed texture and excellent draping qualities. It creates a dressy look for dresses, pants/coat ensembles or separates.

Flannel: A fabric with a soft, plain or twill weave and a slightly napped surface in wool or cotton. In wool, it is best for jackets, slacks and other sportswear. In cotton, it is best for pajamas or nightgowns.

Gauze: This thin, sheer loose weave is one of the coolest, lightest fabrics around. It is good for casual/chic separates or dresses.

Georgette: A sheer fabric; it is soft and fluid and feels slightly crepey to the touch. It is good for dressy wear.

Intarsia knit: A colored design knit into a solid background. It is usually found in sweaters.

Interlock knit: A smooth, firm knit with the same texture on both sides of the fabric, although jacquard patterns are sometimes printed. It may be cotton, rayon or silk.

Jacquard: A method of weaving or knitting patterns right into the fabric, although occasionally they are printed. It may be cotton, rayon or silk.

Jersey knit: A fluid, smooth-textured knit in a plain stitch. It may be cotton, silk or man-made such as acrylic.

Laundered cotton: A fabric that has been washed at the manufacturing stage so it is very soft and looks un-ironed. It is meant to stay that way, so ironing is unnecessary. It should be worn for casual wear.

Linen-look: This crisp, plain-weave fabric has a slubbed, slightly coarse texture. It looks like natural linen but without the wrinkles. It creates dressy daywear or casual/chic separates.

Oxford cloth: A lightweight, soft fabric made in a small basketweave with a smooth surface and a very "breathable" quality. It is used primarily as a blouse or shirt fabric.

Pique: Small, raised geometric designs give this medium-weight fabric extra crispness and body. It is used for dressy daywear.

Polished Cotton: A cotton-type fabric with a glazed finish that adds smoothness, stiffness and luster. It creates a daywear to summer evening look.

Poplin: A very fine rib weave distinguishes this hard wearing, medium weight fabric. It is tightly woven and is used for shirts, slacks and dresses.

Ramie: A natural fiber that looks and feels very similar to linen. Lustrous and absorbent, it is usually blended with cotton for extra softness. It creates casual/chic or daywear looks.

Rayon: This lustrous, soft yarn is found blended with many other fibers, or alone in a smooth lightweight weave. It creates casual/chic or dressy daywear looks.

Seersucker: This lightweight warm-weather fabric alternates smooth and puckered stripes for a crinkled effect and offers true no-iron ease. It creates causal or daywear looks.

Sweater knit: Generally, a heavier weight than other knits. The texture can be flat, cabled, ribbed, pebble, etc.

Tissue Faille: Similar to "faille" but smoother, lighter and silkier. It is used for dressy daywear looks.

Viyella: A blend of 55% wool and 45% cotton. It is wonderful for shirts, skirts and dresses.

9
Let's Go Shopping!

Closet Organization

If you have lots of clothes, but never a thing to wear, then this chapter will help you. A successful image is based on many individual components. When it comes to shopping, one key component is DISCIPLINE. Discipline means staying true to your:

A. Color Palette (the best colors for you)
B. Lifestyle (choosing clothing which best suits your lifestyle)
C. Body Type (correct lines for your figure)
D. Clothing Personality (your personal style)
E. Budget

A successful image and discipline go hand-in-hand.

The second key is to take a physical inventory of your existing wardrobe. It starts with being honest with yourself.

■ Does it honestly still fit well? (We may not have gained a lot of weight over the past few years, but our body weight does shift as we age.)
■ Have I honestly worn it during the last year?
■ Is it honestly in my color palette?
■ Is it honestly in style as to line, color and fabric?

Just remember, the average woman wears 20 percent of her wardrobe 80 percent of the time. What are you doing with the other 80 percent?

Try on any garment in question. If it has excellent fit, style, quality and you have been using it as a key part of your wardrobe, but the color is wrong, look for a good accent color in your seasonal palette which compliments and extends the usefulness of the piece. Example: A camel suit (wrong color) accented with a purple blouse and purple accessories (right color). Just remember, never spend good money on a bad investment. In other words, if you had to buy accessories in a wrong color to make the camel suit complete as an outfit, then it is time to pass the garment along. Be sure your clothing dollars take you as far as possible in what they will buy.

The third key is choosing the three dominate colors that will coordinate with each other. These are known as your "basic wardrobe colors" from which you can build your wardrobe.

Examples include:
Winter
- Red
- White
- Black

Summer
- Gray
- Pink
- Gardenia White

Spring
- Camel
- Ivory
- Coral

Autumn
- Forest Green
- Mustard Yellow

- Tomato Red

These basic colors are used for the base garments we work our wardrobe around - suits, coats, jackets, skirts, or pants. These are your key garments from which you build your wardrobe. Your base colors can gradually increase from three to six. Anything more than six base colors begins to defeat the purpose.

After you establish your three base colors, you can then choose your secondary colors or accent colors. Often you will be surprised as to how much you may already have in your wardrobe which meets the above criteria. We often overlook the obvious because of the clutter. Now is the time to "de-junk" your life. Eliminate the closet confusion. Get your closet down to the garments you really want.

The fourth key component is to evaluate the style of your clothing. Consistency is the secret to a good image. For example, do you have garments hanging in your closet that have hardly been worn because they just never seem to suit the occasions of your life? Do you have a hodge-podge of styles, but only a few garments you really feel good in? Place your focus on a garment you like and feel good in and start building from that point.

Just as a footnote, the clothes that are creating the clutter are often hard for some people to eliminate for a variety of reasons - sentimental value, good quality, "just as soon as I lose weight," and even the memory of how hard it was to earn the money to pay for them. Whatever the reason might be for not wanting to part with an item, the important thing is to remove them from our functioning closet.

Now you are ready to organize your workable wardrobe.

The fifth key is putting your clothes in a functional order. This means that spring/summer clothes are stored separately from fall/winter clothes. Twelve-month items remain year-round. Arrange like items together - all jackets together as well as skirts, blouses, dresses, etc. This will provide a greater visualization of your clothing potential.

The final key is to make a list of the items that you need to purchase to extend and update your seasonal wardrobe. This should include shoes, handbags, and other items of accessorization.

Now we are ready to go shopping! Let's discuss the Do's and Don'ts.

DO!

1. Do go shopping with a good mental attitude. Don't start with focusing on all the things you don't like about yourself, such as not being thin enough or not having an un-limited bank account. Instead, put your focus on looking the very best you can with your existing resources.

2. Do focus your attention on specific stores or departments within stores based on your style, color palette, and budget. If you walk into a department store with no direction in mind, it is easy to become overwhelmed by the "ocean of options." What all too frequently happens in these situations is we walk in and walk out without buying anything we like. Over the years, I have heard most of my clients say, "I've looked in this store before and I never saw any of the things you have brought to me." The only difference between my shopping techniques and my clients is "FOCUS."

3. Do be sure you have purchased and have in place in your wardrobe your key basic garments. This is where it all starts. It may not be the most exciting part of purchasing your wardrobe, but remember: the cake is the base, the frosting is what gives the cake its uniqueness.

4. Do make sure the majority of your purchases build off your key best basic garments. It is better to have five outstanding outfits and feel good and look terrific everyday, than to have a closet full of clothes that you do not feel comfortable in.

5. Do shop with a fashion season, even if it costs a little more. You will be paid back in the time you save.

6. Do shop in coordinate separates whenever possible. This will help you develop a complete look with less time involved.

7. Do buy fit, not size. In today's market, sizing consistency does not exist. It would not be unusual for you to have four sizes of clothing in your closet which appropriately fit your existing body shape.

8. Do consider hiring a private wardrobe consultant if you do not have the time or do not like to shop. Recommendation: Choose a private individual who does not make his or her profit by the amount of clothing you buy. In other words, if he/she is affiliated with a department store, you will be limited to the resources that store provides.

9. Do take advantage of sales, but not necessarily to build your key wardrobe. Sales are an excellent way to add filler pieces or finishing pieces to your already established wardrobe.

10. Do beware of the fabric and workmanship in a garment. A price tag is not always an indicator of quality.

11. Do develop a long-range plan whenever possible that will allow you to buy your key garments at one given time within a season. In other words, save the $500 and purchase your look! This will accomplish several things — provide a more consistent image, save time and save money.

12. Do, when purchasing separates, be sure they create balance in color, line and weight for a "total look."

13. Do unbelt garments such as coats, dresses, jumpsuits, etc. before trying them on; then put the belt on the garment at your natural waistline. Many times we reject a garment for the wrong reasons.

DON'T!
These are the hidden destroyers of a successful image!

1. Don't buy something just because it is a good deal. This whittles away at your clothing dollars, a well as your total image.

2. Don't piecemeal your image. A little bit here; a little bit there is a good way to find a few items to complete your look, but not a good way to develop your base wardrobe.

3. Don't spend good money on a bad investment.

4. Don't choose clothing that requires maintenance or skills that you don't have. For example, you cannot afford a lot of drycleaning bills in your budget, or you do not like to iron, but the garment requires pressing each time it is worn.

5. Don't take all the fun out of shopping by

under-preparing for the event.

6. Don't buy the main outfit and then try to find the right shoes or accessories to complete it. Check first to see if appropriate accessories are on the market. (The fashion industry does not always work together.)

7. Don't shop out of frustration. In other words, don't put your garment needs off until the last minute. When you do this, you sabotage your clothing budget and ultimately your clothing image.

8. Don't buy a garment if you know you do not have enough money left to complete the look. Don't buy a garment if you don't have the correct pieces to finish the look. For example, don't buy a long skirt when your full-length coat is shorter than it is.

9. Don't lock yourself into a mindset. Finding what you like may mean adapting to what is available in the stores at a particular time.

Principles of Process

Random shopping certainly has value. It is intended to provide us with an overview of what is current in the marketplace, who is carrying what items, prices, etc. Random shopping is also a good way to pick up accessory pieces or a "fill-in" item to extend your existing wardrobe. But, if the majority of your shopping is done in this manner, then you begin to sabotage your wardrobe and sacrifice a successful image.

Serious Shopping
First of all, reduce your frustration by being prepared.

1. Be organized! This means have a goal in mind when you start out. Have your closet list, color swatches and your samples of garments in your existing wardrobe.

2. Study the current marketplace. Develop a good sense of comparative shopping. If time permits, check the same products in different stores; prices will often vary. Keep in mind that discount stores are not always a big savings.

3. Use the mail order resources, fashion magazines, and your local newspaper for current fashion ideas. Most newspapers publish pertinent fashion information on Thursdays and Sundays; check your local paper for publishing dates.

4. Become familiar with name brands and quality. Price is not a total indicator of quality, but it can guide us.

Remember, sometimes we are paying for the designer's name and other times we get the best of both. Poor quality decisions will cost us more in the long run. Don't be fooled by a garments affordability. You should strive to gradually upgrade the quality of your garments.

5. Know your resources and what they have to offer. Where can you get the best quality and service for the amount of money you have to spend.

How To Work Within A Budget

Many women shop in a piecemeal manner. An article of clothing here; an item on sale there. It is much easier to justify a $50 expenditure than it is a $500 one. But all too frequently, a piecemeal approach will be one of the major destroyers of a successful image. You will best establish a clothing budget by looking over your checkbook stubs, charge slips, etc. from the previous year to determine what you have a tendency to spend on a given season's wardrobe. Often you will be amazed at how much you actually spend. When you are organizing your budget, be sure to allot dollars to finish the outfit. These are for your accessories.

Always buy the best quality you can for the amount of money you have to spend.

Conclusion

If you have read the various chapters in this book, you are now acquainted with the necessary aspects of developing your personal style. No secrets have been withheld! This means you now have all the needed tools to begin except one, and that one comes from within yourself. It is your attitude. Carl Lagerfeld, designer for the House of Chanel, says "Style has nothing to do with beauty or age. It is ageless and it is an attitude of the mind." A woman who inspires others because of her look does so because of the attitude she has about herself.

If age has nothing to do with good personal style, which by the way is also confirmed by a recent finding that states, "Ageless beauty has arrived in the 90s", then I believe part of the necessary attitude is ageless. A woman with this attitude never thinks of herself as growing older, only improving. She is always young at heart, growing as a person intellectually, emotionally and spiritually for God created each of us with these attributes and they need to be developed.

As you begin your venture to put your new found image together, remember the statement: "It's a process." It does not come together overnight or in a week. You will still make mistakes, but definitely fewer. With each passing season, you should feel better about yourself and the choices you have made, unless your style or color was just not available. That will happen from time to time.

Review some of the sound advice in Chapter 8 on a regular basis. This will help to keep you on track and avoid some of your past pitfalls. Failing to plan is planning to fail. No longer can any of us afford to piecemeal our wardrobe or shop haphazardly. The cost is too great!

I wish you success in your planning and fun in your shopping so that the end result will be...**"All Together You!"**

All Together Me...Personal Style Development

Seasonal Classification:
_____ Winter
_____ Summer
_____ Spring
_____ Autumn

Hairstyle Preference:
_____ Controlled
_____ Wash 'n Go
_____ Latest Style
_____ Feminine/Sexy

Body Type/Frame:
_____ A-Frame
_____ V-Frame
_____ H-Frame
_____ 8-Frame
_____ Combination Frame

Lifestyle:
_____ Professional
_____ Sales/Retailing
_____ Network Marketing
_____ Advertising

Best Colors:
_____ Wear brights, darks & contrasts
_____ Wear all colors equally well
_____ Wear pastels to brights

Hair Color Preference:
_____ Natural
_____ Frosted (cool blonde)
_____ Warm Highlights
_____ Cover Gray

Figure Flaws To Disguise:
Examples: short neck, heavy arms

_____

_____

_____

_____ Homemaker/Mother
_____ Athletic/Outdoors
_____ Entertain Frequently
_____ Crafts/Painting

Clothing Personality: Example: Classic/Dramatic

_____ / _____

Best Fabric Patterns For My Personality Combo:

_____ Solids, florals, polka dots or soft abstracts
_____ Solids, abstracts, polka dots or stripes
_____ Bold geometrics, ethnic, abstracts or solids
_____ Solids, plaids, stripes or paisleys

Best Manufacturers/Designers:

Shop brands for their fit and personality, and then note them here so as to remember what will work best for your look.

Separates (i.e. Chaus)

_____

_____

_____

Dresses (i.e. Susan Bristol)

_____

_____

_____

Shoes (i.e. Van Eli)

_____

_____

_____

Catalog and Store Sources for "My Brands":

_____

_____

_____

Bathing Suits (i.e. Cole)

_____

_____

_____

Lingerie (i.e. Lillyette)

_____

_____

_____

Accessories (i.e. Anne Klein)

_____

_____

_____

_____

_____

_____

If you would like more information on color and personal image seminars contact either:

■

Bette DeHaven
c/o **Designer's Touch**
P.O. Box 8440-156
Westminster, CA 92683

■

The Crowning Touch
P.O. Box 412080
Charlotte, NC 28241-8834

For additional books, order through your distributor, local book store, or write to:
Internet Services Corporation,
P.O. Box 412080, Charlotte, NC 28241-8834.
Please include $5.00 shipping and handling.